REACH THE TOP
in
NEW HOME and
NEIGHBORHOOD
SALES

Myers Barnes

MBA
Publishing

REACH THE TOP
IN NEW HOME & NEIGHBORHOOD SALES

Published by MBA Publications
P.O. Box 50
Kitty Hawk, N.C. 27949

Printed in the United States of America
10

Library of Congress Catalog Number : 99-93301

ISBN: 0-9654858-3-8

Cover and page design by One-On-One Book Production, West Hills, California

Table of Contents

Acknowledgments

No one goes it alone. Everyone needs someone and I am proud to say that every one of my accomplishments has been blessed with the valuable help of many giving people.

First, I want to thank the companies and organizations that took the chance and employed me, starting as salesperson up through Vice President of Sales: Fairfield Communities, ShipsWatch, Barrier Island Station, and Bob DeGabrielle and Associates. Each career move was a valuable learning experience and the company owners, management, and staff were critical links to my development.

Second, I recognize my unending debt to each individual and company who has ever been in my audience, read my material, or listened to or viewed my tapes. Our experience together has proven invaluable for me in the creation of this new book.

I thank my mentors: Brian Tracy, Bob Schultz and Nido Qubein. Your influence—through your books, tapes, conversations, letters and examples—has meant the difference between failure and success, and has fueled my desire to teach.

My greatest heartfelt thanks goes to my family who has given understanding, support and encouragement to my sometimes obsessive pursuits and exhausting work schedule.

To my loving wife, Lorena, my best friend and partner: I am a fortunate man, and I appreciate you more than I can express.

To my creative son, Hunter, who has appeared unexpectedly twice, first at birth, then at our doorstep: Thanks for showing up. You're always an inspiration.

To my Mother, whose self-made mission in life has been to give unselfishly to her children.

And to God, who has made all things possible.

Preface

Have you ever given serious thought to what a book is? A book is an exposed mind. Once you take it down from the shelf and crack it open, you become miraculously linked, mind-to-mind, with the author.

Once linked, at your fingertips are years of research and experience from not just one mind, but countless minds. That is how it is with this book. Aside from knowledge gained through my own experience, between its covers you will find information that has been extrapolated from the minds of some of the greatest people in the sales profession. Their best strategies were distilled and simplified to be included in this one condensed volume.

I know there are those who do not like to read. This is evidenced by statistics from the American Booksellers.

- 70 percent of Americans have not visited a bookstore in five years.

- The average American reads less than one book per year.

You would think no one would choose illiteracy. Yet, as Mark Twain said, "The man who does not read good books has no advantage over the man who cannot."

The seed of wisdom is the realization of how little we know. Most brilliant people who excel in their professions are not impressed with how much knowledge they have, but with how much they still need to learn.

What is a know-it-all? A know-it-all is someone who believes he or she knows all there is to know about his or her subject.

How can you tell who are know-it-alls? Simple. They have stopped learning and growing in their professions. Those who think they know it all live under the delusion that there is nothing new to learn and to implement in their careers. This failure to seek new information places them in an *unconscious intelligence trap* that stunts their growth.

Dr. Albert Einstein once gave a final exam to an advanced graduate class in physics at Princeton University. After administering the exam and on the way back to his office, his graduate assistant challenged the brilliant professor by asking if he had just given the same test he had given the previous year. Einstein readily acknowledged he had indeed repeated the same exact test, which lead his assistant to ask, "How could you give the same test two years in a row?"

Pay close attention, because Einstein's answer holds a profound truth. Einstein replied, "Though the test was the same, the answers have changed."

This is an important point. In our profession, it should remind us that the strategies we employed last year in our sales and marketing efforts may be outdated and untrue today.

Have you, your team, or company fallen into the *unconscious intelligence trap* and stopped growing? Or are you employing methods and strategies that may have worked in the past and perhaps even now, but may not carry you forward into the next century?

Don't make the fatal mistake of believing there is nothing new to learn, or that you already know it all, because personal development, commitment to excellence and being the best in your field is akin to running a race with no finish line.

Your education, which probably began with a set of blocks, should go on as long as you do. And it should include benefiting from the experiences of others.

Don't be as the person Samuel Taylor Coleridge described when he wrote, "To some men, experience and education are like the stern lights of a ship, which illuminate only the track it has passed."

Thank you in advance for your eager, open and receptive mind. May you be enlightened.

Introduction

Red Motley is famous for having said, "Nothing happens until a sale takes place."

Think about that. The salesperson sells cars, tractors, radios, televisions, refrigerators, computers, homes, health and leisure products, ambition and fulfillment. By knocking on doors, answering phones, responding to questions, and demonstrating products and services, he or she enriches billions of lives. Without them, there would be no American ships at sea, no busy factories, and no jobs. Everywhere they go, they leave people better off.

If we were to stop selling, someone would stop buying. If someone stops buying, then someone else stops making. When someone stops making, someone stops earning. And when someone stops earning, they stop buying.

So you see, as a salesperson, you are very important to the productivity and success of this country. In addition to that, nothing happens for your company until you sell a home or a home site in your community. When you do, everyone, from the stockholders, to the president, to the support staff, to your own customer, benefits from your sale. At the same time, you flip on a switch activating the factories across the world that determines the entire direction of the economy.

In 1997, an article in *Forbes* magazine included these calculated statistics: The average American salesman keeps 33 men and women at work—33 people producing the product he sells—and is responsible for the livelihood of 130 people.

Every economic indicator makes reference to the level of sales in a particular company or industry. Our stock market and price indexes center around the goods and services being sold at any given time, and you, as a salesperson, fuel the entire social and economic process. Impressive.

Besides powering the economy, many of you also help others find the American dream of home ownership.

As a new home/new community sales professional, you are involved in what I consider to be the single most important profession in our country. You help people make one of the most significant decisions of their lives—specifically how they will live their lives.

Regardless of whether your community represents a primary residence, a second home or a retirement home, you are helping people select the environment that they trust will mold and shape their own lives and those of their families.

Before you can help them, however, you might need a little help yourself in knowing how to be more effective in new home and new community sales. The purpose of this book is to teach you a process that will make more of your sales "take place."

In reading, you will find that several points are repeated throughout the book. There is a reason for this. A person must read or hear the same thing several times before it begins to register in the mind. You'll learn more about that in the book but, for now, I'll simply say that I practice what I preach.

This book includes everything you need to know to lead your buyers into purchasing their new homes from you. May you open it with expectations and close it with a profit.

1

CHANGE IS YOUR *ONLY* CONSTANT

Whatever you do, or dream you can do, begin it. Boldness has genius, power and magic in it.
~ Johann Wolfgang von Goethe

I find the great thing in this world is not so much where you stand as in what direction you are moving. To reach the port of heaven, we must sail sometimes with the wind and sometimes against it, but we must sail, and not drift, nor lie at anchor.
~ Oliver Wendell Holmes

✍   ✍   ✍

Today you are in a unique position to accumulate and enjoy all the rewards that new community/new home sales will offer in the future.

To do this, however, you must begin a journey. One that will *increase* your sales, *improve* your income, and *involve* you in merging your dreams with reality.

There is a catch, of course; or rather, a condition: In order to experience an improvement of any kind, you must be willing to do something different. In other words, you must be willing to make certain changes in your life.

Change is necessary, but not necessarily easy. As the expression goes, "Many are called, but few get up." Brian Tracy says, "We want things to stay the same, but simultaneously get better. Yet nothing stays the same, and situations and circumstances are always going to

1

change, some for the better, some for the worse, but they *will* change."

In simple words, change is inevitable (unless, of course, you're trying to get it from a vending machine).

SOCIETY'S FEARS

In my seminars and corporate training sessions, I ask the audience what the three greatest fears in our society are today. Although there are a host of fears from which to choose, surveys have shown that the three greatest fears, in order of priority, are:

- public speaking
- change
- death

Though it seems unrealistic, public speaking is ranked as society's number one fear. Think about it. If you were asked at this very moment to get up in front of an audience of 15 or 500 to deliver a speech, how would you feel? For a few, public speaking is comfortable, but for most, it's terrifying, and many will never attempt to conquer this fear.

However, if you think it's strange that people have such a hard time dealing with public speaking, consider the next conclusion. Those surveyed actually preferred death to change!

Now you are probably thinking, "That's ridiculous! Who would rather die than change?" Using myself as an example, I will prove to you that change, for most of us, is so threatening that death is often preferable.

Several years ago, I smoked cigarettes and, at one point, was consuming about two packs per day. Now, consider the incontrovertible facts: Smoking systematically kills. It has been reported that every time we inhale the chemicals and nicotine from one cigarette, we are taking approximately 14 minutes off our lives.

So, by continuing my habit—two packs, forty cigarettes a day—I was saying that I would rather die prematurely than change.

Of course, there are other unhealthy habits that lead people toward an early grave—over-indulgence in food or alcohol, drug use, destructive relationships, laziness or inactivity, and even excessive use of the computer can lead to depression and other ills.

Admittedly, we all have areas of our lives that we should work to improve. But we don't. Instead, we keep repeating the bad habits and wondering why we don't make any headway. To paraphrase Dr. Albert Einstein, *to do the same thing over and over and expect a different result each time is insane.*

The reality is that our lives are constantly changing; but, unfortunately, all change is not growth and all movement is not forward. Life is continually in a state of flux. As the Bible points out, all things will pass. Nothing stays the same. We are either improving or declining, going forward or backward, becoming freer or more addicted.

It is the doctrine of entropy, meaning that if you are not putting energy into something to make it better, it is going to get worse. This law applies to anything in the universe. Look around you. If not maintained, paint peels, metal rusts, wood rots, cement crumbles, teeth decay. The same principle applies to relationships and people, brains and businesses. If unattended, they deteriorate.

A tidal current runs through our lives, but that tide is not the Gulf Stream. It does not flow in only one direction. Instead, it is like the ocean. There is a rhythm to each day—an ebb and flow—a coming and going—that we need to recognize and ride. Our lives change; either we control and influence those changes or they control us.

What does any of this have to do with community sales? Everything! Our profession is evolving and rapidly changing. What may have worked in the past will hinder our progress in the years to come.

Answer the following questions:

Q   If I continue to operate my business in the same fashion today as I did yesterday, what will be the result?

If you continue to do things the same way, you can expect the same results. Is that what you want?

Q   Even if today I am a successful on-site sales professional, if I continue selling as I am now, are there sales I am missing?

Be honest. Could you be loosing one sale a week or one sale a month by continuously conducting your business the same way, day in and day out?

The point is, you cannot expect to do business today the same as you did yesterday and get better results without implementing some changes.

To change is to be willing to be uncomfortable for awhile and to close old doors in order to open new ones. But I promise, as you change to adjust to the industry's tidal flow, and grow and evolve into a more polished and professional new community sales representative, it will be worth it, because you will increase your sales, improve your income and fulfill your dreams.

There is joy in beginning. Start now being different than you are.

DIRECTING CHANGE

If change is inevitable, how do you cope with, or more importantly, manage it? There are three key words that will influence your degree of success. Those words are *inclination*, *expectations* and *education*.

1. Inclination. To control the changes that enter your world, you must position your mind correctly. What slant do you put on life when it unexpectedly swerves or throws you a curve? Do you automatically lean toward the negative or the positive? What is your attitude? Are you excited, thrilled and elated? Or are you upset, fearful and frustrated? Do you expect the worse and make the worst of it when it happens? Or do you awaken to a world full of rainbows and silver linings? Do you see a rock pile or envision a cathedral?

> *It's your attitude not your aptitude that determines your altitude.*
> — **Zig Ziglar**
>
> *To the dull mind, all of nature is made of lead; to the illumined mind, the whole world sparkles with light.*
> — **Emerson**

We all know we should have a positive attitude and focus on what is good. We've read it and heard it repeated in every sales education and motivational program. But what exactly is attitude? Simply stated, it is how you position your mind toward a person or thing. It involves your thoughts, feelings, disposition, emotions, opinions, expressions. It is your attitude in life that determines your approach to life. It subconsciously dictates, "This is how I view things, so this is the direction I will take."

A friend of mine who owns a printing company knows that, when the printing press is operating, he must carefully watch what is being produced. If tiny pieces of paper adhere to the plates, or the ink balance becomes incorrect, or the image isn't aligned properly, the final result is a print job that is "off registration." He could end up with an unwanted, out-of-focus image stamped repeatedly on pounds of paper.

That's how our minds are. We are continually having images stamped on them. If we don't watch what we're thinking, we may, as Lord Buckley observed, "Suddenly wake up and realize there's a strange picture on our press."

In his book *The Leader in You*, Dale Carnegie wrote, "I was asked once on a radio program to tell in three sentences the most important lesson I ever learned. That was easy. 'The most important lesson I have ever learned,' I said, 'is the stupendous importance of what we think. If I knew what you think, I would know what you are, for your thoughts make you what you are. By changing our thoughts, we can change our lives.'"

Whenever I consult with company sales managers, I conduct an exercise on how to recruit a new home/new community sales associate. Since they are managers, I stress that their incomes are not based on the results of their own personal sales, but exclusively on the sales of the associates under their guidance. Therefore, they should concentrate on the ongoing recruitment and motivation of a world-class team of professionals. They are then asked to sum-up in one word the best attitude or characteristic they would want from a new recruit in assembling this exceptional sales team.

Using three columns as indicated by the diagram, the managers then volley back and forth listing what they consider to be the most important traits a salesperson should possess.

Figure 1.1 Characteristics of a Superachiever

CHARACTERISTICS	ATTITUDE	SKILL
1. Honesty	➼	
2. Integrity	➼	
3. Commitment	➼	
4. Motivation	➼	
5. Industriousness	➼	
6. Cheerfulness	➼	
7. Loyalty	➼	
8. Self-discipline	➼	
9. Punctuality	➼	

The characteristics most often mentioned are honesty, integrity, commitment, motivation, industriousness, cheerfulness, loyalty, self-discipline, and being punctual.

After completing the list, the participants are then asked to check in the appropriate column whether each characteristic of the super salesperson is an attitude or a skill. You'll notice, after reviewing Figure 1.1, the characteristics of a Superachiever normally center around the person's attitude.

Of course, there's always the question, "Shouldn't we recruit experienced salespeople when assembling a world-class team?" Ideally, we would all love to have a team of experienced professionals working for us. However, it's worth noting that **experience is not necessarily an indication of one's ability or knowledge.**

Many times experience only refers to the amount of time on a job. If someone has ten years experience, but has a negative attitude and has not absorbed any new information (from books, tapes, seminars), then his experience may be only one year times ten. Frequently, managers prefer salespeople with years of experience to new recruits with the proper attitude. That can be a costly mistake.

2. Expectations. The second way to control and benefit from change is to make your expectations high.

What causes one person to be optimistic and another one to be pessimistic when confronted with the same situation? It is their expectations. Those who expect outstanding results will be naturally positive and optimistic. Having confident expectations is a key quality all top new home/new community sales professionals possess.

Once during a corporate training session for a Fortune 500 real estate company, Guy, a top producer, asked, "Myers, does this mean you believe we can actually *will* a customer into ownership?"

I answered, "Guy, suppose you were in your car driving to an appointment and for 30 minutes prior to your appointment, you verbally repeated affirmations such as, 'I'm happy to serve, and my prospect excitedly awaits to own my new home.' All the while you visualize the successful consummation of the sale.

"Now let's consider another scenario. This time you're driving to your meeting. You affirm mentally and out loud, 'This appointment will not go well. They are looking at three other neighborhoods and just want information and brochures.'"

Directing the question from Guy to the group, I asked which of the two mental and verbal rehearsals would increase the probability of a sale.

In unison the group responded that rehearsing the positive affirmations and visualization versus the negative ones would enhance the sale's success.

> *If you think you can or think you cannot, you are right.*
> — **Henry Ford**

Driving to the appointment with a great attitude and the expectation of a positive outcome does not guarantee a sale; however, it certainly increases the probability of one, and is much better than throwing some brochures at the prospects and telling them to call if they're interested. As the proverb urges, "Once you've gathered your materials for a temple, don't build a tool shed." Go for what you want, and expect to get it!

Often, when conferring with community representatives prior to their appointments, we formulate a precall strategy to get this positive energy flowing. The first question I always ask is, "What homesite have you selected for them to own?" (or) "What home do you plan on helping them acquire?" Usually I receive a reply such as, "Well, I don't think they will own today," or "This is their first visit. I'm just giving them information at this time."

Do you understand what occurs with this type of attitude and mindset? The salesperson's mental expectations predispose him to the outcome he expects, which is for the sale not to occur. On the flip side, when expectations are high, salespeople will *make* more opportunities than they *find.*

An ambitious young man ventured to ask a wealthy industrialist what his secret of personal success was. The rich man replied, "There is no secret. You just have to jump at your opportunities."

The young man responded, "But how will I know when these opportunities come?"

"You can't," the rich man said. "You just have to keep jumping."

It is imperative that you determine your goal, lock into your mindset, and "keep jumping" with the expectation of achieving what you really want. Otherwise, you would have to conclude that you really don't want it in the first place.

Just like the homes you sell, your career needs an architect, someone to follow a blueprint and build, out of the materials on hand, the kind of life you want. That architect is you.

Every day you will shape your future. Although nobody else can do it for you, there are many who will influence it. If, in building, you aim for the heavens, your life and your work will resemble the temple and not the tool shed.

> *Even when we're in the gutter, some of us are still looking for the stars.*
> — Oscar Wilde

3. Education. Education is the final key ingredient to managing change. It is the yeast that causes attitudes and expectations to rise.

> *Education is the ability to listen to almost anything without losing your temper or your self-confidence.*
> — Robert Frost

Now, what do you think the difference is between a professional and an amateur athlete? I ask this to individuals and audiences on a regular basis. Normally, the reply is that the difference is the money they are paid. This is only partly true, but the suggestion cuts to the heart of the matter.

The major difference between a professional and an amateur is not the amount of money they are paid, but the amount of time that they practice. Period.

Let's explore the training schedules of some of the highest paid athletes in our time. Professional boxer George Foreman was quoted in *Selling Power Magazine* as saying, "Train hard, fight easy." He should know. He has a grueling schedule. Though his conditioning normally occurs year round, to get himself in peak condition ten weeks before a fight, Foreman runs behind a pickup truck for two-and-a-half hours everyday. While running he intermittently weaves jabs, punches and ducks, simulating action in the ring.

Ten miles down the road he fits himself into a harness and drags the truck back for half a mile. Foreman's motto, which also speaks to anyone striving to be a champion in sales, is, "Training should be harder than reality."

While we're on the subject of boxing, Muhammad Ali once said it was the preparation to win that determined the outcome in the ring. "The fight is won or lost far away from witnesses. It is won behind the lines, in the gym and out there on the road, long before I dance under those lights."

Once you realize that the average Olympic athlete invests 1,200 days of practice for one day of competition, you begin to understand that the major difference between a pro and an amateur is indeed practice.

> *If you don't do your homework, you won't make your free-throws.*
> — **Basketball great Larry Byrd**

Practice is an inner-drive, a commitment to excellence, to being the best. When fathers drag their seven-year-olds up to Wayne

Gretzky, the Mozart of hockey, and say, "Wayne, will you tell him he's got to practice?" Gretzky responds, "Nobody ever told me to practice." The same is true for Tiger Woods. Not once did Earl or Tida Woods insist their son get in his golf practice. With Tiger, the trick was getting him to come home.

So what does practice have to do with education? Well, it's a natural consequence that the more we practice, the more we learn about our craft and ourselves. And the more we learn, the better skilled and the better educated we become.

Now, let me pose another question: In regards to new home/new community sales, do you consider yourself a professional or an amateur? Before answering, remember the difference between a professional and an amateur athlete is practice. So how much are you practicing? Specifically, have you reduced your presentation to writing? Do you rehearse it? Do you role-play your presentation and closing strategies with your manager or other committed team members? Do you regularly read books and trade magazines, listen to tapes, or attend seminars about sales, real estate, marketing, and personal development?

We revere those professionals who have achieved greatness by practicing and becoming so good at what they do that they eventually win the coveted "cup." It is the fact that they are disciplined enough to practice day in and day out—to subject themselves to what I call "repetitious boredom"—that distinguishes them as professionals. Yet, it never seems to occur to average salespeople that they, too, must educate themselves and practice if they want the unlimited rewards that a career in real estate sales offers.

Consider the following fact: Knowledge and information in our industry, and for that matter in any industry, is doubling (and changing) every two to three years. This is significant news. As Jack Welch of General Electric has observed, "If change is greater on the outside of your business than it is on the inside of your business, then the end is near."

I applaud you for the fact that you are investing your time and sharpening your skills by reading this book. But understand, though this book is a solution, it is not the final answer. Your training and education must be ongoing. Part of your formula for success should be to consume a steady diet of good information, which will help you not only stay current in the marketplace, but also earn a professional's income.

What are the ingredients for this diet? They are the same ones that were given to me several years ago and have now been delivered to thousands of professionals just like you.

First, you must **invest financially in your education**. Expect to set aside three percent of your gross income toward your personal development. For each $100,000 you earn, invest $3,000 in you. When this suggestion is presented in seminars, the immediate response of many participants is that they can't afford this. However, they say, once they make the money, then they will contribute to their education. We will review this later, but for now realize that this is a commitment that must be made prior to experiencing the result.

Second, you must be willing to **invest your time.** This is a two-fold commitment. First, you must discipline yourself to read one hour per day in your field of business. Although the mind is a muscle, I have yet to figure out how to hook-up a Nautilus machine to it. Therefore, the best way to strengthen and nurture your mental muscle is by reading.

> *Man's mind, stretched to a new idea, never goes back to its original dimensions.*
>
> — Oliver Wendall Holmes

If you read one hour per day, you will average reading 35 to 50 books a year. Do you think if you read that many books in a year you would begin to stretch your mind and improve your skills?

The second part of your time commitment is listening to motivational training tapes and CDs.

An average salesperson will spend many hours of travel time in a car every week. By attending "Automobile University," as we call it, you can turn this downtime into productive time by listening to inspiring speakers transmit ideas meant to exercise that mental muscle of yours.

The third and final way to digest information is to **frequent seminars, programs and workshops** conducted by industry leaders. One of the side benefits of attending these is that they expose you to other professionals, just like you, who may be already earning and achieving more than you are. As you have opportunities to speak with them, you can "pick their brains" to see how they arrived at where you want to go.

Pay attention to the words of Jim Rohn, the business philosopher. "Work as hard on yourself as you do on your job," and I guarantee you will excel in the ever-changing profession of new home/new community sales.

In closing, here's a poem to ponder.

It's Time to Change When...

When you suspect you're going wrong,

Or lack the strength to move along

With placid poise among your peers

Because of haunting doubts or fears;

It's time for you to shift your pack,

And steer upon another track.

When wind and waves assail your ship,
And anchors from the bottom slip;
When clouds of mist obscure your sun,
And foaming waters rapidly run,
It's time for you to change your plan
And make a port while you still can.

When men laugh at your woeful plight,
And tell you now to end the fight.
When all the world bestows a frown,
While you are sliding further down,
It's time for you to show your grit,
And let the doubters know you're fit!

When failure opens your luckless door,
And struts across the creaking floor;
When Fortune flees and leaves you bare,
And former friends just coldly stare,
It's time to take a different tack,
And show the world you're coming back!

2

THE MODERN RULES TO SELLING

All the world is a store, and all the people in it are salespeople. That is to say, every one of us is trying to transfer an idea from his own head into some other brain. And that is the essence of salesmanship.
~ Arthur Brisbane

The salesman who thinks that his first duty is selling is absolutely wrong. Selling is only one of the two important things a salesman is supposed to do, and it is not the more important of the two. The salesman's first duty is to make friends for his house.
~ Ellsworth M. Statler

There are more goods bought by the heart than by the head.
~ Myers Barnes

Like technology, professional selling has been evolving and changing more rapidly in the last few years than in any other time in history. It used to be all that was required to achieve a sale was a single call, to a single buyer, with a single product.

Remember the day of the door-to-door salesman? He typified the old method of selling.

Perhaps you've heard the story about Mrs. Calvin Coolidge, who found it hard to say no to a persistent book salesman. Long before her husband became president, a fast-talking door-to-door salesman convinced her to buy an expensive medical book on home remedies. Because she was reluctant and embarrassed to tell her husband how much she spent, she hid the book around the house and tried to keep it out of sight—he never mentioned it.

One day, however, she picked up the book on home remedies and happened to glance at the flyleaf. There, in her husband's handwriting, were these words: "Don't see any recipes for curing suckers."

Today we have veered away from the door-to-door, one-product salesman and evolved into a multi-market selling society. For a salesperson, there are many more factors to consider, such as quality, financing, price, amenities, and add-ons or incentives. The competition can be just around the corner or anywhere on the World Wide Web. Our customers are bombarded with a sea of new communities and countless new home ownership opportunities. They are overwhelmed with details, options, upgrades and choices.

Start with your marketplace, for instance. If you are involved in new home sales, how many competing communities and builders are chasing the same consumer in your particular geographic range? Or, if you represent resort/retirement communities, consider how many other options your customer has outside the immediate area. It's possible the consumer is driving an entire coast or mountain range seeking the one perfect offering.

It has been estimated that the average home or homesite purchaser will visit as many as five to 12 communities before making a decision. Personally, I think this is a conservative estimate, and would suggest that the number of communities visited is only limited by the number of communities available to view in a particular marketplace.

Consider the following statistics from the November 1997 issue of *Professional Builder*: "58 percent of our customers will contact two to four builders, 25 percent will contact five to seven builders, and 17 percent will contact between eight and fifteen builders. This is compounded by the number of models and floor plans they will view, and the number of on-site salespeople they must wade through before reaching their final decision."

Of course, let's not forget the number of brochures, renderings, price sheets, covenants, and even video tapes doled out at each of their visits, and you can easily see that the process of onsite sales is much more complex than it has ever been before for both the customer and the salesperson.

THE NEW MODEL OF SELLING

Acknowledging that community sales is a sophisticated business and the consumer's options are unlimited, it becomes obvious that to compete successfully, you must employ a selling procedure that adapts to current conditions.

Happily, there is such a procedure, and it will be your key to increased income, superior sales, and, more importantly, a greater degree of satisfaction in your sales career.

Refer to the accompanying diagram (Figure 2.1). The upright triangle represents what is called the Old Model of Selling. The inverted triangle represents what has come to be known as the New Model of Selling.

Models of Selling

Old Model of Selling

Figure 2.1

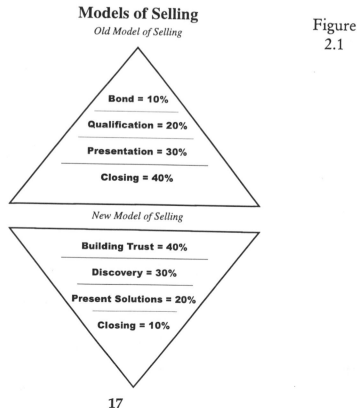

Bond = 10%

Qualification = 20%

Presentation = 30%

Closing = 40%

New Model of Selling

Building Trust = 40%

Discovery = 30%

Present Solutions = 20%

Closing = 10%

THE OLD MODEL OF SELLING

In the early 1900s, the first organized form of sales training was conceived. At that time, what was taught was totally appropriate, because it was what the customer responded to favorably. This basic form of sales training and presentation style proved so effective, it was the training-of-choice for virtually every sales organization in the country.

The Old Model of sales training divided the sale into separate portions, as Figure 2.1 reflects. Salespeople were taught that they needed to spend 10 percent of their time (at the top of the triangle) finding a common ground and building a bond with the prospect. This was normally an insincere combination of flattery and small talk in which the salesperson discussed the kids, the trophy on the wall, current sporting events, a recent vacation, or whatever. It didn't matter what subject, as long as it proved to be a common ground that would foster bonding.

After forming the bond, the salesperson would move to the second portion of the triangle. This was the qualification phase of the sale to determine if he or she "had a live one." It was quick and to the point. Normally the prospect was asked, "If I could... would you... ?" types of questions; specifically, "If I could show you the best deal of your life, would you take advantage of it now?"

If the prospect replied "no," and the salesperson played the number's game, he or she simply moved on to the next person, continuing this until the day's quota was reached. However, if the prospect replied "yes," then the salesperson latched on with a python-like grip. The customer was hooked.

Finally, the sales procedure slid into the third quadrant of the triangle—the sales pitch. This represented 30 percent of the time invested with the prospect. Let's analyze the word "pitch." According to Webster, pitch means to heave, and heave means to throw-up.

That's certainly an interesting concept. Have you ever had a salesperson "throw-up" on you? Have they heaved so much material and information your way that you felt overwhelmed?

Here's the point. First, drop the word "pitch" from your vocabulary. And second, don't toss a brochure at potential customers, thinking they can read all about the new homes and communities themselves. This is the mark of a non-professional. You should either be in front of a prospect or working to put yourself there.

Now, back to the triangle and the Old Model of Selling. While engaged in the sales pitch, the salesperson would talk his customers to death with a features-and-benefit type of presentation. There was very little interaction because, once the salesperson was on a roll and in a rhythm, the customer was almost forced to sit back and listen. The conversation became a monologue, not a dialogue.

Having invested 30 percent of the selling time in the sales pitch, and having succeeded in verbally knocking the customer senseless, it was now time to enter the final quadrant of the triangle—the close.

The close represented 40 percent of the sales process. Normally the salesperson had memorized countless closing techniques that forced customers to make decisions and literally manipulated them into buying something that frequently they weren't able to afford, couldn't truly use or enjoy, or did not need.

Now, I have a question. How would you feel today if you were a customer and this Old Model of Selling was the process used to present a new community and home to you?

The Old Model of Selling, still being used today by some song-and-dance salespeople, adheres to the principle that sales is a numbers game. If you see enough people, you will make enough sales. Period. It isn't about people. It's about quotas. They believe selling is something you *do* to someone versus *for* someone. Viewed this way, selling becomes an unfriendly procedure with unnecessary problems.

Thank goodness a revolution and transformation occurred in the 1970s and ushered in a new selling procedure that, when applied to new home/community sales, becomes your ticket to incredible sales performance.

THE NEW MODEL OF SELLING

The New Model of Selling, like the Old Model, recognizes sales as a procedure, but that is the only similarity. Notice the New Model (Figure 2.1) is also illustrated by a pyramid, but the proportions of each quadrant have changed, flipping the triangle upside down.

Beginning at the top of this pyramid, 40 percent of your sales process is invested in building trust. Because our prospects are inundated with opportunities to buy countless communities and model homes, and are confronted with an infinite number of real estate salespeople, trust must be in place as the cornerstone in the sales relationship. Without question or compromise, you must sell yourself before you sell your product.

It is the level of trust between prospect and salesperson that provides the cohesiveness necessary to establish a solid relationship and begin the sales process. And it is your responsibility to produce in your prospect the confidence to buy.

How do you build trust with your prospect? I suggest several ways:

1. **Know all about the new homes and community you are selling.** Your primary objective is to assist your prospects in making one of the most important, life-altering decisions in their lives. Don't take this responsibility lightly. The more knowledge you can provide the buyers, the more they will learn to trust you and request your input.

2. **Speak their language.** One of the attributes of people who have charisma is that they match their tone, language and speech speed to those with whom they are talking. Doing this yourself will make customers relax and become comfortable dealing with you.

3. **Be confident.** Always assume the prospect is going to buy from you; if not now, then later.

4. **Honor your word.** When you keep your agreements, it says you trust yourself. But don't make the mistake of expecting everyone else to keep theirs. This leads to frustration, anger and disappointment.

5. **Maintain a good reputation.** It is the best advertisement for a professional salesperson. In 1953, when Ben Hogan was trying to establish a golf equipment manufacturing company, he meticulously created each set of golf clubs himself, striving to make them as near perfect as he could. Disregarding advice from friends to go ahead and put a product on the market he felt was inferior, he destroyed $150,000 worth of golf clubs before he finally perfected one good enough to carry his name.

6. **Listen.** This is probably the most effective and simplest way to develop trust with a prospect. How do you listen? It's simple. You ask questions, which brings us to the next portion of the triangle—Discovery.

My greatest strength as a consultant is to be ignorant and ask a few questions.

— Peter Drucker

Listening is learning. Listening allows you to discover what the prospect needs, and to learn why your prospect wants a new home. Is it for profit, to be used as rental or investment property? Are they looking for security? Status? Pride of ownership? Have they been renting for a while and are now looking to become part of a community? Are they moving up in the world or scaling down? What is their passion? At this point in their lives, what is motivating them?

On the subject of listening, think about how many ears you have. That's right, you have two. Two ears, one mouth. This not-so-subtle message is that you have been created to listen twice as much as you talk.

In a sales presentation, when you listen to your prospect, it prevents you from talking too much, and it encourages your clients to voice their needs.

Referring again to the first portion of the New Model, invest 40 percent of your time in building trust. The surest way to build trust is to listen your way (versus talk your way) into the soul of your customer.

To repeat two profound points:

1. **Telling is not selling.** You listen your way into a sale with the New Model, whereas you talked your way with the Old Model.

2. **Questions are the answers.** The best way to get the answers you want is by asking questions and listening responsively.

Discovery involves uncovering your prospects' agenda and gaining knowledge of their unique circumstances as they relate to your community and the new homes and homesites you offer. To do this effectively, you must question skillfully using well-prepared scripts. Then listen attentively, focusing on your customers' perception of their reality. Recognize that you are the liaison between the new home and the mind of your prospect. You must know both before you can serve either.

Of course, you don't want to become *The Interrogator,* and wipe them out with questions. You do, however, need enough information to match your customers to the new homes best suited to their needs. By asking questions you can determine where they are now and where they want to be. This will also help them crystallize their thinking.

If you are following the New Model of Selling, by now you have invested 70 percent of your time in building trust and discovering what your prospect wants and needs in a new home. You have done all this before even attempting to deliver your sale's presentation.

Since you are focusing 100 percent of your attention on the customer, you are no longer the typical salesperson but are accelerated to a trusted advisor, partner and personal consultant. Your prospect now feels you are investing in this decision with him and, although you are not making a financial contribution, you actually join your prospect in the role of assistant buyer.

Now move into the third portion of the triangle—your presentation. This constitutes the 20 percent of the New Model of Selling, in which you are able to prove to the prospect that his or her lifestyle needs can be satisfied by your community.

The final portion of the triangle is the closing— gaining commitment and consummating the sale. Instead of the close being the agonizing part of the home-buying process, disliked by both the salesperson and the customer, it becomes the natural ending to a great presentation.

One final point concerning closing. Do not think, "Oh, good! I am closing the sale." Instead think, "Great! I am beginning a long-term relationship."

Your primary aim in new home/new community professional selling is to first position yourself as an advisor by helping your customers with decisions that will benefit them; and second, to build a meaningful referral relationship—the lifeblood of your future business.

If you help enough people get what they want, you will always have what you want.

— **Zig Ziglar**

3

THE BUYING PROCESS

Coming together is a beginning. Keeping together is progress. Working together is success.

~ Henry Ford

One must learn by doing the thing, for though you think you know it, you have no certainty until you try.

~ Aristotle

People will buy anything that's one to a customer.

~ Sinclair Lewis

❧   ❧   ❧

Brian Tracy compares a professional sales process to a combination lock. The numbers of a lock are synchronized and in perfect order. When the combination is dialed in the proper sequence, the lock will easily open.

This analogy is applicable in new home and community sales. Our customers shop by a process. If we can understand their standard buying procedure, then we can develop a method of selling that will coincide with it.

TOP CONSIDERATION FOR A CUSTOMER IN A BUYING DECISION

Countless hours and dollars have been spent through the years in an attempt to identify and understand the "average shopper." The conclusion is that there seems to be three central factors in the shopping process that buyers consider.

First is the product. Our tangible product in its condensed form consists of the community, homesites and homes. Later in this book we will delve deeper into more complex issues facing the buyer, but for now you need only be aware that your product is a central factor in the customer's decision-making process.

The challenge with our communities, homesites and homes is that frequently the consumer regards us, collectively, as homogeneous in nature. This means that, at first sight, they view us all the same. When you think about it, this isn't surprising. After all, how else are they to view our communities? Every developer, builder, and marketer advertises and boasts fundamentally the exact message: Their neighborhoods are the best with great homes, great warranties, great lifestyles, and, of course, great prices. Consequently, to the would-be homeowner, we are all initially created equal.

The second factor our prospect considers is the **company** representing the products (community, homesites). Though every effort is made to bolster confidence with the developers and builders, there is a subconscious fear the consumer faces when selecting the seller.

By giving thoughtful attention to the trends in business today, you can understand why homebuyers have deep-seated concerns about companies from whom they are about to make the single largest investment of their lives.

According to current statistics, 80 percent of all business start-ups will fail within the first five years of opening their doors. Aside from failed small business start-ups, during a ten-year period ending in 1990, the success rates of Fortune 500 companies weren't too impressive either. During that time, 157 companies tumbled off the big board's list and more than 100 additional companies folded, merged or changed their ways of doing business. This indicates to consumers that no company, regardless of size or strength, is safe.

We must also consider the volatility of our industry and face the reality that we have our own performance challenges. Consumers are also scrutinizing developers, building contractors, and real estate firms.

There is a trend in our business to offer the one-year new-home warranty, with appliance and fixture manufacturers giving longer-term guarantees. Unfortunately, the subtle message consumers consider but don't always convey is that they do not question the home's life span, but the company's. Will it be around long enough to make-good on those warranties and guarantees?

The final factor customers consider in their buying process is the **salesperson** who represents the company and the product. According to studies at the University of Illinois, 68 percent of the consumer's decision to own centers around the salesperson. This is a conservative figure, because other studies reveal that up to 80 percent of the buying decision is influenced by the salesperson. Why? Because, before any customer will invest in building or buying a new home, he or she must invest in building a relationship with you, the salesperson.

You actually serve as a gatekeeper, bridging the gap between your customer and your product. Consequently, your customer will find something wrong with what you're selling when your customer finds something wrong with you.

To the consumer, you are the only true barometer of the neighborhood and the homes. This is crucial information for developers and builders, who should make certain their sales force reflects the proper image. The consumer will judge the company not only by its product, but also by its people.

THE CUSTOMER IS IN A HURRY

Now that we understand how shoppers evaluate our products, companies and salespeople, we have a better idea of how their minds work when they are entering the buying process.

How many prospects have walked into your sales office or model home center and tried to prevent an actual conversation by saying something such as: (1) "I'm in a hurry. I just want a brochure." (2) "My husband is out in the car. I need a price sheet, plat and floor plans." (3) "I'm on my way out of town (or) to the airport." (4) "We were driving by—I would just like some basic information about your neighborhood and homes."

These comments are typical of those that may initially introduce you to potential customers.

Keep in mind, however, that before they ever walk out their front doors and into yours, they will probably look at a dozen or more advertisements for new home communities that seem to fit their basic needs. Then, while driving to the various home sites, they are blitzed with billboards, banners, flags, and signage from competitors that entice them to view their "open houses" and "models."

If that isn't overwhelming enough, at each community customers are faced with multiple "preferred" builders, each showcasing three to five homes, and a waiting-at-the-door sales staff ready to pounce. It's no wonder our customers have such a tough time making a decision. There's so little time and so much from which to choose.

To make it even worse, we live in a do-it-now society accustomed to instant gratification. Despite all of our conveniences, we appear to have less time to ourselves than our forefathers did.

All of this makes for an anxious customer, one who is feeling pressured, confused, and in a hurry. Is it surprising then that the average buyer tries to find an easier way to shop?

SHOPPING BY THE PROCESS OF EXCLUSION

Throughout this book there will be revelations that undoubtedly will make a significant difference in your career. The following should be one of them.

Homebuyers today shop by the process of exclusion. They are looking for reasons to exclude your community and homes, rather than reasons to include them in their buying process. They want to *cross you off their lists*. Therefore, your goal should be to become the only choice they have by demonstrating that any other alternative is out of the question.

In an interview, Grateful Dead founder Jerry Garcia explained the reason he felt his band and its music had such longevity. "You do not merely want to be considered just the best of the best. You want to be so good that you are considered the only one who does what you do."

Why do people shop by exclusion? Because they get tired of thinking, looking and comparing. Either they feel they don't have the time or don't want to take the time to explore everything available in the marketplace. So, if they can find a reason to cross you off their lists, they'll do it.

It's like watching television. Remember when we only had the networks NBC, CBS and ABC, and maybe a local public television station? Back then, it wasn't hard to choose what to watch because the options were so limited.

Today, with the advent of satellite television, we have more than 150 stations at our fingertips. By touching a button on the remote, we can flip forever.

The next time you look through the television guide, pay attention to how you choose the program you'll watch. Because there are so many, you will probably do as most of us do: mentally skim over and eliminate those you have no interest in watching. When that happens, you are actually shopping for a program using the process of exclusion.

Here's another example: You are dining this evening in a fine restaurant. In your hands is an incredible menu offering nine captivating appetizers, six delectable salads, and more than twenty prize-winning entrees including beef, chicken, lamb and seafood. You have the option of selecting any number of items from the thirty-five listed on the menu. Any choice would be delicious and would satisfy even the most discriminating palate. Even though they all sound good, your stomach only holds four to five cups of food, so you can't possibly eat them all. How do you decide?

Using the process of exclusion, you scan the menu, mentally rejecting those dishes that are least appealing. Perhaps you do not indulge in red meat, so you eliminate beef and lamb entrees. This leaves five seafood and six chicken dishes. You had chicken last night, and you don't want it two nights in a row, so it's excluded. This elimination process continues until you arrive at what you consider the one perfect meal for the evening.

THE SELECTION OF A NEW COMMUNITY

The selection process for new home communities works the same way. Because there are so many choices, customers begin eliminating their options. They may cross a community off the list because it's too close to the city or too far to drive; too congested or not developed enough. The homes may be too small for comfort or too large to heat; lacking closets or having carports. The customer may object to the lifestyle, the neighborhood, the price and even the paint.

Then, of course, there is the salesperson. Maybe the customer encountered one who was unfriendly, having a bad day, selling according to the Old Model, not attentive, unprofessional or in too much of a hurry to do anything more than deliver a handout.

Believe me, customers will find plenty of reasons to cross you off their lists; the foremost being simply because it's one less property to consider.

This is one of the reasons the process of Discovery is so important. By listening to the customer, you can justify why your community should be included in the buying process before he can find grounds for it to be excluded.

4

THE SALES PROCESS

People give me credit for some genius. All the genius I have lies in this: When I have a subject in hand, I study it profoundly. Day and night it is before me. My mind becomes pervaded with it. Then the effort that I have made is what people are pleased to call the fruit of genius. It is actually the fruit of labor and thought.

~ Alexander Hamilton

◆◆◆ ◆◆◆ ◆◆◆

THE PROFESSIONAL APPROACH

A professional is someone who is engaged at an elevated position in an advanced occupation. Professionals have a standardized set of business practices and conduct their businesses with sound systems and processes from the first step to the last.

Professional on-site selling is a complex process involving discovering, influencing, and overcoming the natural buying resistance that all shoppers have until they become customers. Sales is not an easy profession. The myth in our business—that community sales is easy if you just see enough people—is lethal to a salesperson's success.

Builders or developers who delude themselves into believing that selling is easy and strictly a function of traffic, then transfer that concept to their sales teams, will be beat like a drum in the marketplace.

It does not matter how many people (prospects) you see in a given day. What counts is what are you doing with the people you see.

You will begin to move yourself forward into the upper ranks of salespeople when you start to approach your business as a profession that strategically centers its activities around a sales process with standard systems.

SELLING TO A PROCESS

There will be thousands of new business start-ups today. All of them can be lumped into two distinct categories. First is the franchise, and second is the non-franchise.

The failure rate for the non-franchise is staggering—fewer than 20 percent will survive for more than five years. On the other hand, one of the fastest growing areas of business start-ups is the franchise, which offers a systematic way to profitably operate one's own business.

A franchise is a form of licensing by which the owner of a product, service or method obtains distribution through affiliated dealers. The International Franchise Association, the industry's trade association, defines it as "a continuing relationship in which the franchiser provides a licensed privilege to do business, plus assistance in organizing, training, merchandising and management in return for a cash consideration from the franchisee."

Currently, around 94 percent of those who invest in a franchise are successful. Why so many? Because those who invest in a franchise are not only investing in a business, but are also investing in a proven success system. There is minimum risk and maximum opportunity for success by utilizing the established product or service and marketing method. In other words, follow the process to the letter, administer the system, and if it's an appealing franchise in a good location, you will be successful.

The amount of investment for a franchise can be a few thousand dollars or more than a million. Regardless of cost, heed the wisdom of business consultant Peter Drucker. "You are only in business as long as you can afford your mistakes." The successful franchise has already made its mistakes and can now offer a replicable business process with proven systems that enable duplicable sales on a consistent basis.

Here's a thought-provoking exercise for you. Describe your community sales process, as you know it. If, for even a moment, you are pausing or do not have the slightest idea what the process is, it's understandable. Most salespeople, except for an elite few, respond the same way.

When interviewing a prospective community sales representative, I always say to him or her, "Please describe the new community sales process as you know it."

Then I wait, hoping they will give me an abbreviated version of: "Well, I have to first meet and greet my prospects as they enter my sales center/model home. Then, through the process of discovery, I will determine their wants, needs and desires as well as their financial ability to own. Afterward, I will give them a brief overview and presentation, covering the highlights of our community and our builder(s).

"From here, I would demonstrate our homes and homesites with my entire goal being to have them select 'one and only one.' Of course, it is imperative that I create a burning sense of urgency that prompts my prospects to take action today.

"I realize a new home is the single largest investment in most people's lives, so objections and concerns will probably surface. My job is to have anticipated their objections in advance so I can calmly and confidently handle them and then close and consummate the sale.

"Nevertheless, in spite of the best sale's process, my prospect may not decide to own in my community today. Therefore, I outline the necessary follow-up procedures that will secure the continuing appointment and I will stay in touch until my prospect becomes a customer.

"Once they become my customer, I enter the follow-through portion of the process. The sale remains in progress and I facilitate the details until they take delivery of their new home/homesite, because a satisfied customer will provide me with an endless stream of referrals."

Once the sales representative has concluded, I will ask him or her, "Well, what if the customer tells you he really needs to think about it? How do you respond?"

If the sales representative doesn't give me an immediate answer, knowing that "I want to think about it" is the most common objection, then I know we have a lot of training to do.

Also, if the salespeople I'm interviewing don't say that they will follow up with me, I know they won't follow up with the customer either.

How about you? Can you describe the community sales process as you know it? Are you able to answer in a manner similar to the one described in the previous scenario?

If not, that's OK, because the rest of the book is dedicated to providing you with a proven process to use in new community and new home sales. If utilized, it will bring you a greater chance of success, just as a franchise would if you were buying a business.

At this juncture, it is important you understand what a process is; specifically, "a *process* is a series of actions and *systems* directed toward an end result."

A process can be applied to anything. When I was writing this book, for example, I wrote according to a process. First I researched and organized my material. Then I outlined the points I wanted to make. From them, I wrote a first draft. And finally, I refined it until the end product was complete.

In sales, a process with systems causes you to sell on purpose and your business will be duplicable because your actions are repeatable.

The process is like a tool and, as with any tool, it must be handled properly. When it is, selling that is based on a customer-friendly process is one of the most effective ways to influence and initiate change.

SCRIPTS AND DIALOGUES

The nucleus of the community sales process consists of scripts and dialogues. You control the *process* (not the customer) by what you say, how you say it, and when you say it.

In this book, you will be given a powerful, comprehensive collection of proven strategies used by renowned sales stars, including real-life scripted situations and actual dialogue that you can use to gain an immediate advantage and to achieve more sales.

Successful salesmanship is 90 percent preparation and 10 percent presentation. You can't sell until you're ready to sell. Otherwise, it is simply the customer making a decision to buy. **So, before you present, you must prepare.**

You communicate your presentation by *words*. Your words paint visual pictures of the opportunity you are offering during the sales process. The average salesperson sells poorly because he or she does not take time to master the presentation, including a planned "sales dialogue."

You are probably familiar with the term "arts and sciences." In the community sales process, you shouldn't practice the art—that is the correct method of expression–until you study the science—the systematic knowledge. Once you've mastered the system, then you can express it.

Consider the professional actress. On screen, her performance seems effortless. That's because backstage, unseen, she has been memorizing her script and practicing her stage delivery. Only after mastering the science (the script), does she practice the art (perform).

Remember, selling is a skill and, as with any skill–whether it's acting, riding a bicycle, or playing a musical instrument—it is only mastered with practice and rehearsal.

COMMON OBJECTIONS FROM SALESPEOPLE

When instructing future Sales Superachievers to learn their scripts and dialogues word-for-word, many resist. Following is a list of their most common objections.

■ *Some of the scripts and dialogues will not work in my operation, or some clash with my personality.*

That's understandable. Use what's comfortable for yourself and for your operation, and build your sale's presentation on what's adaptable.

■ *The scripts and dialogues are not my words, yet you expect me to learn them word-for-word.*

I jokingly tell salespeople, "Of course they are not your words. It's my name, not yours, on the front cover of the workbook."

I ask you to learn the techniques word-for-word first, and then, over time and after practice, you will adapt them to your own conversational style. This is the process of making something your own.

Several years ago a student approached me with a notebook of his favorite closing techniques. Essentially, they were the same techniques I had shared, yet after he had memorized the original ones, he rewrote and adapted the strategies to suit his selling situations and personality. He expressed to me, with delight, that learning the scripts had actually made his job easier and his sales higher.

■ *The sales process and memorization are a lot of work.*

I understand. I fought it, too. But think of the alternative. Refer back to Chapter 1, "Change Is Your Only Constant." If you continue to do business in the same manner, what kinds of results can you expect? If you continue to operate the same way, you can expect the same results. Remember? Is that what you want?

You must expect to pay the full price in advance to experience the success you desire, and that price is hard work. As the expression goes, "Many like to sit under the shade tree, but few like to rake the leaves."

For me to mislead you by promising that success should come easily, will destroy your enthusiasm and cause you to give up at a later date once you find it isn't true.

When Henry Ford was listening to workers bemoan having to learn something new, he responded, "There is no man living who isn't capable of doing more than he thinks he can do."

The entire object of true education is to make people not merely do the right thing, but to enjoy doing the right thing; not merely to be industrious, but to love industry; and not merely to be learned, but to love knowledge.

— Educator John Ruskin

Memorizing isn't easy, but it is educating you in the best way to sell. It is saying, "Apply this process because it has been proven to work." And, hopefully, by doing this, you will find more enjoyment and success in your chosen career.

One last bit of advice: As with any type of art, there has to be some place to draw the line. And this is it, with *no exceptions*: **First you memorize. Then you personalize.**

Don't deviate. Selling to a process is like writing music. At some point, you can compose by ear, by feeling or by instinct. But first, you had better know the rules and the notes because they provide the guidance you will need, especially when you feel you're getting nowhere.

NOW IT'S TIME TO GET DOWN TO BUSINESS

On the next page, Figure 4.1 outlines the Power Process for Community and New Home Sales. The Power Process has ten steps. Each step will be covered comprehensively and explained in detail in the following chapters. It is suggested that you earmark the following page as an easy reference to the sequence of events in the Power Process.

In reviewing these steps, you might begin to yearn for the end result, which is Closing the Sale. And rightly so, since our very existence in the profession of selling is validated by closed transactions.

However, the Power Process is a sequential progression of events that is in perfect order. Although the selling process is essentially a closing process, to get to the end (closing), you must have the discipline to start at the beginning. The following chart gives you a brief overview of the 10-Step Power Process. Each step will be discussed in depth during the following chapters.

> *The Power Process causes you to sell more rather than less—sooner rather than later.*
>
> **— Myers Barnes**

THE POWER PROCESS

```
                    Meet & Greet
                         |
(*Simultaneous)   *Discovery | *Present & Overview  <----  Urgency
                         |
                    Demonstration  <-------
                         |
               Selection of the
                 "one of a kind"
                         |
                  Overcome objections
                         |
              Close
                         |
                       Follow-up
                         |
          Follow-thru  ---->  Referrals
```

5

PREREQUISITES OF THE POWER PROCESS

We should have the will to do, the soul to dare.
                                        ~ Sir Walter Scott

The will to succeed is important, but what's more important is the will to prepare.
                                        ~ Myers Barnes

❧   ❧   ❧

One of Murphy's Laws is, "Before you do anything you must do something else first." What this means is that there is always something else to do before we can start to do what we want. Then to make it even more of a challenge, when we try to prioritize what we want to do, sometimes the last thing we know is what to put first. Confused? Let me get specific.

In learning the Power Process and prioritizing the steps, we recognize that there is something else that must be done first. In fact, before beginning the process, there are three essential psychological conditions that you must understand because they occur during the Power Process. These are **enthusiasm, fear** and **urgency.** Any attempt to sail through the process without fully understanding these psychological conditions will greatly reduce the effectiveness of your selling.

ENTHUSIASM

Why do people buy? When we ask this question, we usually receive what seems to be logical answers.

1. It's the right price. People may think they are shopping price, but they actually buy based upon what their *perception* of value is. They will choose to own what they think is the best value, which frequently is not the lowest-priced item.

If a customer truly desires your neighborhood and homes, you may rest assured that cost will not be the final factor in this—*the most significant decision of his or her life.*

2. It's what we need. Our needs are basic and few. Our wants and desires are unlimited and unquenchable. We always want more than we need, because our wants and desires are emotional, whereas our needs are logical.

Your customers will select the neighborhood and purchase their new homes for emotional reasons, and then attempt to logically justify their decisions. The aspects of price and terms are logical explanations, and salespeople and consumers alike believe we become involved because of these. But in truth, consumers will not be making the purchase of their new homes or homesites based on logic. As a matter of fact, if you hear someone say that it was the "logical decision," he means he had more of his emotions invested in reaching the logical conclusion.

We are emotional beings and every choice in life is flushed through emotional levels prior to reaching the logical surface. We become excited first and then we rationalize our decisions to own by saying something was the right price or was just what we needed.

HOW WE SHOP—WHAT WE BUY

In truth, shoppers think they are buying a product, but they are actually buying a feeling, a perception. For example, *you* sell books. *They* buy knowledge. *You* sell insurance. *They* buy security. *You* sell computers. *They* buy convenience. *You* sell homes or homesites. *They* buy the feeling and perception of satisfaction that your community's lifestyle promises. New communities and homes are not commodities, but vehicles to dream fulfillment. That house may represent the joy of achievement, the comfort of belonging, the thrill of independence.

40

They aren't just buying a house; they are buying their homes. It is here that they may get their first look at marriage, family or civic responsibilities. From here conversations, impressions and attitudes will be formulated and shared. This home will become a school where lessons of truth or falsehood, honesty or deceit, are learned; and it will pattern the smallest structure of society known as the family. Your customers may choose the shape of the house, but it will ultimately be the home that shapes them. Isn't it exciting to realize you have a very important part in all of this?

Because the buying decision for a new home and neighborhood is based on emotions, your degree of enthusiasm about your product will affect your buyers...not to mention your career, your company, and your confidence. And, since buying decisions begin at an emotional level, selling means transferring your enthusiasm into the mind and the emotions of the buyer. A salesperson minus enthusiasm is just a clerk.

Look at the last four letters of enthusiasm. IASM means I Am Sold Myself. Your customer is unable to become emotionally involved until you deliver your presentation with a white-hot excitement that ignites your prospect's interest. To be able to persuade your prospect, you must go beyond simply knowing your product to truly believing in and loving the worthwhile benefits and solutions your community and homes offer. You must:

1.   Believe in what you sell.

2.   Believe your prospect will profit by it.

3.   Believe in the firm you represent.

One of my seminar attendees approached and told me that she lacked enthusiasm. There were issues of credibility surrounding her community and, to complicate matters, she was disenchanted with the quality of service her company offered. My advice to her is the same I give to you. If you do not believe in your company, community, and homes, and if you wouldn't own one yourself or recommend it to your best friend, then you are involved with the wrong neighborhood and builder. If this is the case, do yourself and everyone involved a favor, and have the courage to make a change. Otherwise, you will never develop the enthusiasm needed to succeed in helping your customers with such a significant decision.

In your mind's eye, picture an empty cup. Now, pour water into this cup until it is full. Next, picture your prospect possessing an empty cup prior to viewing your community and homes. Since a sale is a transfer of enthusiasm, you must visualize pouring the contents of your cup into his cup. But you can only pour in the amount you have.

FEAR—IT WILL SABOTAGE YOUR SUCCESS

We have discussed the positive elements of a sale: attitude, confident expectations, and enthusiasm. Now, it's appropriate to analyze what will be happening to you and your prospect during the sales process. Remember the process of transferring your enthusiasm to the emotions of the prospect? Just as you are capable of sending positive emotions, so you are also capable of transferring negative emotions—feelings that will block your sale.

The fear of failure is the greatest single obstacle to success in adult life. Our fears make us reluctant and anxious and they well up inside us whenever we are faced with risk or with doing anything new and different. This is especially true when it involves selling a major lifetime investment, such as a home.

During the sales process your prospect will experience tensions and negative emotions. This is known as "buyers remorse in advance." She can experience this even if you have transferred 100 percent of your enthusiasm and confident expectations. Whenever your prospect reaches the crossroads of decision, the point where she must commit to either a yes or a no with your community, and she is not 100 percent certain she is making the right choice, she will experience her greatest fear—the fear of failure.

The prospect's fear of failure rivals the fear of making a mistake. We have all made buying mistakes, such as purchasing products that did not meet our expectations or paying too much for something.

When "buyers remorse in advance" overwhelms your prospect during the sales process, she will procrastinate and vacillate rather than commit and make the decision to proceed. She makes predictable statements such as, "I'm just looking," or "I need to think it over," or "I need to discuss this with my banker, accountant, attorney or family." But what the prospect is truly saying to you is, "I'm experiencing buyer's remorse in advance and am afraid of making a mistake."

As if the buyer's fear isn't enough to prohibit the home sale, there is also the salesperson's fear of rejection and hearing the word "NO" during the sales process.

More than anything else, it is probably this fear of rejection that is holding you, as a salesperson, back. It is the fear of rejection that causes you to withdraw from your prospect. And it is this fear of rejection that you must overcome if you are going to experience greatness in sales.

Why is it we fear rejection and the word "NO?" Because it is an acquired fear that has been taught to us throughout our lives. Psychologists tell us our fear of rejection and "NO" stems from childhood. As babies we enter into the world without fear or preconceived notions. Through unintentional destructive criticism, our parents and figures of authority teach us our fears.

Ever hear the phrase "terrible two's?" Of course, today educators have put a positive slant on it by calling it the "terrific two's." Regardless of its title, it is that stage of life in which babies begin to explore, to reach out and touch anything they can. The second year of life presents a world of exploration and adventure. During this age children must be carefully watched by their parents or they could easily hurt and even kill themselves.

So how do parents and guardians teach and train their children? By repeating "NO!" By the time children are past their second birthdays, they will have heard this word thousands of times. ("No, don't do it." "I said no." "No, put that down." "Stop it," etc.) Often a parent will have reinforced "NO" with a little pain, such as a slap on the hand or pat on the bottom. Findings concur that by the time the average child reaches adulthood, he or she will have experienced the word "NO" somewhere between 116,000 and 148,000 times. Is it any wonder we fear rejection and hearing the word "NO"?

Salespeople would benefit by understanding that the "NO" they hear is nothing more than a knee-jerk reaction by the prospect.

When you sense yourself fearing rejection from a prospect, tell yourself that fear is nothing more than **preparation energy that is getting you ready to perform**. And the "NO" you hear is just the natural response you get at the moment of closing when your prospect is experiencing buyer's remorse in advance.

The fear of failure, or of making a mistake, literally has the power to drive both you and the prospect into a safer harbor. For the prospect, that protection is provided by saying "NO." For you, the salesperson, that safety comes by avoiding rejection by not asking for the sale.

Here's an example of what salespeople experience daily. A person walks into a new community/sales center looking for a home. The salesperson approaches and says, "May I help you?" Automatic responses are something like: "No thanks, I'm just looking," or "No thanks. I just wanted to see what you have," or "Not now. I'm just looking around. If I have any questions, I'll find you."

A perspective buyer walks into the establishment, literally on a mission to purchase, and the salesperson approaches with, "May I help you?" The prospect's knee-jerk reaction, the natural response, is "No, I'm just looking."

Whenever a prospect is in a position to buy but is experiencing the possibility of a mistake, he will protect himself with the "NO GO" response. He is *not* going into that arena, and he's not giving you permission to take him there. Consequently, he will maintain control of the situation by "just looking."

By the way, if, as a salesperson, you fear hearing the word "NO," you have placed yourself in an interesting profession. The potential of a sale and the possibility of rejection are "joined at the hip." If your closing ratios are 10 percent, you will see 100 walk-in prospects with only ten becoming owners. That means 90 prospects reject your proposals. When the economy is down and competition is keen, you may experience rejection from as many as 95 out of 100 prospects.

So accept it: You will hear "NO" many more times than you hear "YES." The top community sales professional expects it, prepares for it and is able to continue forward by possessing a sound sales process and system.

The final point about rejection is that you cannot take it personally. Realize when people say "NO" to you, they are just offering an automatic response. *They aren't rejecting you as a person.* They are merely saying "NO" to the conditions of the offering such as the location of your community, your designs, the delivery schedules, and a host of situations surrounding your community and homes, but *not to you personally.*

CONQUERING FEAR

Fear percolates through your thinking and makes you the landlord of a terrible tenant. It is like a virus, permeating your body, breeding in your mind, eating away your spirit. But fear can be the first step to something better. With a little more courage and a little more effort, you can have victory.

Here are some suggestions to help you overcome the fear of rejection:

- ❑ **Don't take rejection personally.** Understand it is the prospect's fear of failure, of making a mistake, that prompts the rejection. When you get a "NO," don't be shocked by it. Don't disbelieve it or blame the competition. Instead, accept it, analyze it, and learn from it, then move on—either with that prospect or with another. But don't internalize rejection. It isn't, as the expression goes, "all about you."

- ❑ **Expect rejection.** This doesn't mean for you to be negative. It doesn't contradict the need for confident expectations. It is just reality.Recognize that a sales conversation will usually end

45

with the prospect's refusal or semi refusal. What is a semi refusal? When you are offered objections such as: "I'm just beginning to shop." Or "I'll get back to you later." Or "I need to think about it."

On the average, more than 80 percent of every sale occurs after the salesperson makes five to seven closing attempts. In other words, you must ask prospects to own your homes a minimum of five to seven times before they buy. What's surprising, however, is that 50 percent of all sale's conversations end without the salesperson attempting to even ask for the sale or attempting to close *even once*. (Remember the safe harbor? Avoid asking and you avoid rejection.)

Furthermore, you may expect your prospects to visit multiple communities. Even if they love your homes and lifestyle, because of competition, many times prospects will perform their "due diligence" before making their final selections. By anticipating the possibility of refusal, you are able to structure your sales process, plan your closing strategies, and implement your follow-up campaign.

❑ **Confront your fears.** *Confront* your fears. *Control* your fears. But do not take *counsel* with them. Fear should not dictate your responses. If you face the obstacles, fear fades. You can fear rejection, or have faith in yourself. The emotion you cultivate—faith or fear—is the one that grows.

Do what you fear most and the death of fear is certain.
— **Ralph Waldo Emerson**

Avoid being too hard on yourself while you are working to improve. Expect to feel uncomfortable as you approach the sales process and develop new skills. It is natural to feel uneasy doing something you have not mastered. Through repetitiveness and experience, you will gain the strength, courage and confidence to face and conquer your fear of rejection.

❑ **Overcome buying fears.** In facing your prospects, the first commandment is: *Don't let them scare you!* Remember...they are potential *buyers*. However, they frequently are *indecisive* buyers. Usually indecision and procrastination work on the side of the prospect.

When you think your prospect is being indecisive, then perhaps you have not eliminated all of her fears. Beyond the fear of making a mistake by investing in your community instead of another one, she may also be having a negative response to what you are saying.

All your prospects are a blank canvas when they first enter your model home or sales center. You communicate your presentation by words, which act as the brush that paints the picture of the lifestyle your community and homes offer.

The words you use will either multiply a prospect's fears or elevate his confidence. Negative, fear-producing words will generate negative thoughts, while positive words will generate positive thoughts.

Sometimes it is helpful to make a personal and private evaluation of your presentation. To do this, practice your presentation in front of a mirror. Observe how your face looks, and what your body language is saying when you are facing the customer. Learn to modulate your voice. Make it softer when you are making an important point. Pause when you want to get the listener's attention.

To help in selecting the right words to use, refer to the following chart. The words on the right evoke confidence while the ones on the left are negative and breed fear and skepticism.

DON'T SAY THE WORD:	INSTEAD SAY THE WORD:
Agent: Agent is threatening and provokes a negative thought.	**Representative or consultant:** To consult is to offer helpful advice.
Buy: To buy is to give up security, which is their money.	**Own, acquire, be involved:** People love to own. They don't like to buy.

Cheaper, cheapest: Diminishes value.	**Best value, less expensive, smart money:** Reflects smart value conscience.
Commissions: They do not like to pay your commission as part of the purchase price.	**Fee for service:** Your service always out-weighs the fee.
Contracts: Sounds stiff, formal, difficult and requires the service of an attorney before signing.	**Paperwork, agreement:** Connotation of mutual understanding.
Sign: Never sign anything until checking with an attorney.	**Approve, authorize, endorse:** "Mr. Smith, could you authorize the agreement, or approve the change order, please?"
Problem: Everyone has enough problems. Don't complicate the sale.	**Challenge or opportunity:** We rise to the call of a challenge.
Cost or price: It always costs too much and the price is too high.	**Total value:** Equates with a fair return on the investment.
Deal: "Make a deal" or "Get a deal" sounds shifty. May be too good to be true.	**Value or opportunity:** An investment that leads to a favorable end.
Down payment: A request for security (money). Indicates future payments.	**Initial investment:** The beginning of a positive result.
Monthly payment: People fear incurring more debt and already have enough payments.	**Monthly investment:** Money toward value and profit.
Pitch or spiel: Carnival con man; carpetbagger	**Presentation:** Introduce an opportunity.
Sell or sold: People do not want to be sold to and do not want you selling them.	**Help them to own or acquire:** Get them involved. "Mr. Smith, once involved as an owner, you will enjoy the benefits."
House: Cold and unemotional. A lifeless building.	**Home:** Memories, holidays, warmth, a haven.
Lot: Suggests a tiny parcel or small plot.	**Homesite:** Where they will make the most significant emotional investment of their lives.
Spec: The most negative industry jargon. Speculative represents "built for profit." You establish negotiation with this word.	**Nearly completed home or completed home:** Ground-floor opportunity. "Mr. Smith, our builder's showcase homes are representations that allow you to experience the quality of construction, or give you the opportunity to acquire a completed home."

Condos, units: Only an amateur would say unit. Presents cold, unemotional structures that are connected with apartments.	**Home, residence or villa:** Pride of ownership.
Complex: The very connotation sounds confusing.	**Amenities or facilities:** "Mrs. Smith, let me show you the exciting lifestyle our recreational facilities/amenities offer your family."
Standard: Nothing special, available to everyone.	**Included features:** Position the ordinary (standard) to the extraordinary.
Upgrades, options: Brings to mind, "What is the true value?"	**Special features, customary features:** "Mrs. Smith, the special features allow the opportunity to enhance or personalize your new home."
Left: Suggests "hard to move" homes or homesites.	**Available or remaining opportunities:** Suggests a planned release, saving the best.
Monthly dues, maintenance fees: Has the same impact as paying taxes.	**Monthly maintenance investment or contribution:** Investment toward the integrity of their homes and communities.
Restrictive covenants: Confining and conveys limited use.	**Protective covenants:** Preservation of their investment.
Ups, be-backs, tire kickers: Industry slang adopted from the automobile showroom. Let your prospect hear, "Sam, you're up!" or "Jenny, your be-backs are here," and you will send them running out the door.	**Customer, opportunity, guest:** Our business is the customer, to whom we owe our success.
Punch list, presettlement inspection: Invites them to literally pick the home apart.	**New home orientation:** A time to deliver their warranties and demonstrate how it all works and how they will live, prior to their moving in.

Imagine the following two approaches to the same closing scenario:

The average salesperson asks for the order: "Mr. and Mrs. Walker, this is a great deal, our cheapest unit, and all that's left. It costs one hundred, twenty four thousand dollars. The down payment is 25 grand, and the monthly payment is eight hundred, five bucks. All you need to do is sign the contracts to buy it. Well, what do you think?"

The wise Superachiever asks for the same order in a non-threatening, professional manner: "Mr. and Mrs. Walker, this home is our best value and your final remaining opportunity. The total investment is only one hundred, twenty four thousand, with the initial investment being twenty five, eight, and the monthly investment only eight hundred and five dollars. Mr. and Mrs. Walker, you are making a smart choice for your family, as well as a wise investment. All that's necessary to begin the process is for you to authorize the agreements."

The first scenario is the approach of the salesperson we want to avoid. The second scenario involves a true professional and is more likely to build confidence in the prospect, whereby the couple becomes a customer.

Occasions for Negative Words: There is a moment when you are allowed the use of negative words, and that is when you are being compared to your competition. (The rule is never knock the competition. Every negative statement you make about your competitor's product or service just makes you look bad.)

When being compared to your competitors, you can help yourself by mentioning they have deals, while you offer value and opportunities. Example: "In fact, Sam Smith is a good agent, and the houses in his tract are cheap, but allow me to share with you the lifestyle our community will offer your family and the quality and designs of our new homes."

Remember, your words transmit your ideas and thoughts. Choose words that do not create a disturbance within your customers. Otherwise, your transmission of ideas, enthusiasm, and knowledge may be lost.

A powerful agent is the right word. Whenever we come upon one of those intensely right words in a book or a newspaper or in conversation, the resulting effect is physical as well as spiritual, and electrically prompt.

— Mark Twain

URGENCY: INDUCING ACTION

The salesperson's greatest enemies to the power process are the prospect's indecision and procrastination. It is common for customers to want to procrastinate and most will put off making a buying decision if they feel they have time to delay. As a matter of fact, most prospects will delay even if they know your community and homes are exactly what they want. Why? Because they can.

Personnel consultant and public speaker Robert Half defines postponement as the sincerest form of rejection. He adds that it's a "sure bet that anything delayed will get further delayed."

Hesitant buyers frequently make statements such as:

- Do you have any additional information?

- We're in the initial stage, just beginning to look.

- We need to see one more home. (or) What else is available?

- We need to think it over.

- We must check with our advisors first.

These phrases indicate uncertainty, and a desire to avoid making a decision that the customer thinks can be delayed.

How do you overcome indecision and procrastination? **With urgency.** Awaken your customers to the new home. Arouse enthusiasm. Inspire a vision of what they may become while living there. Reveal what they can do and the value they can have in the community. Lead your prospect to take action today by kindling a fire that creates a sense of urgency, which provokes and incites him to buy *now* before it's too late.

"Too late" means the conditions surrounding the offer will be different at a later date if the prospect decides to procrastinate. "Too late" means the circumstances will not only change, but they may have an adverse effect on the buyer if he delays the decision to own.

The salesperson's most important role is to create and maintain— from the beginning of the presentation to the close—a positive

51

psychological force that helps the prospect maneuver around the emotional barriers that could delay the sale.

Urgency is not high pressure. It is simply conveying the genuine facts the prospect needs to know to make an informed decision during your presentation. Some of those facts may be associated with deadlines and have a certain degree of urgency attached to them.

Review the home's features, the advantages of buying there, and the benefits to the customer of buying *this home, in this community, from you, today*. Perhaps you point out to your prospect that there is a limited availability of homesites, and what you have now will not be available later. Or, maybe there is an impending price increase, and your homes will soon cost more. Or finance rates are lower now than they have been in previous years. Whatever the reason—availability, price or financing—the conditions for owning will not be as favorable as they are right now.

Direct your efforts toward putting your prospects in a frame of mind so they will be moved to action by a given set of facts. This is creating urgency, which can propel your customers through their procrastination and indecision.

The Fear of Loss and Desire for Gain

Your prospect's two greatest emotions are the desire for gain and the fear of loss. Desire for gain is a function of your presentation and how you help prospects perceive through their senses and emotions the lifestyle they will enjoy as a result of owning in your community. The prospect is not so much buying a home or homesite as he is acquiring the perceived feelings of satisfaction or dream fulfillment that can only be realized with your unique offering.

The fear of loss causes prospects to feel they will miss out or lose if they do not own in your neighborhood. Also, people love what they cannot have. As a matter of fact, most people do not even realize how badly they want one of your homes or homesites until it is suggested they cannot have it.

Judy, a top producer in a retirement community, called to say her sales were slow. When questioned as to the cause, she said she felt certain it was because there was no urgency. I asked if she believed a sale was a transfer of the salesperson's enthusiasm to the emotions of the customer.

Judy immediately assured me that her enthusiasm was not the problem. She understood the positive role it played in the sale.

Our discussion continued and centered on the fact that customers sense our emotions. If we are happy and excited, we transfer the same emotions. Likewise if we are negative and fearful, we transfer those emotions.

As we talked, Judy realized that, although she was enthusiastic about her new homes, she was losing sales because she was not transferring that sense of urgency. Her customers were not being motivated either by a legitimate fear of loss or a personal desire for gain. Somewhere in her presentation, she was dropping the ball by not expressing or stressing the limited availability of the homes they wanted to buy.

Urgency is an emotion, and in order for the prospect to have a sense of urgency, we must first *feel it*, then *forward it* to the prospect.

As a salesperson, you must sell to the prospect's emotions. The emotion of satisfaction coupled with the emotion of urgency will determine whether your prospect purchases or not. Top sales organizations are those whose people incorporate the desire for gain with the fear of loss, creating urgency.

There are many ways to convey urgency, but perhaps the most powerful method is to quote actual sales figures. If your community is selling three homes or homesites per week, you might quote the rate of sales at the beginning of your presentation, saying something such as:

Superachiever: "Mr. and Mrs. Prospect, before discussing our homes and the lifestyle our neighborhood will afford your family, you will notice on our community map the homesites that are tagged/flagged in red. This indicates the homesites that have already been sold. As you can see, we are quite busy at (community). As a matter of fact, we have three homes/homesites that are purchased daily/weekly by families/people just like you."

Throughout your presentation you continuously quote your rate of sales, and if your prospects should mention they are far away into the future (30 days) you are able to say:

Superachiever: "Mr. and Mrs. Prospect, as I mentioned, we have three families becoming owners in our community weekly. This means at the end of the month, the availability of homes/homesites will diminish by twelve. I'm happy to show you *today's* best values, but please bear in mind whatever you see today will, in all probability, not be available to you tomorrow."

The above mentioned scenarios epitomize urgency by incorporating the emotional pull from both the desire of gain and the fear of loss. Urgency statements such as these should be conveyed throughout your sales conversation.

SYNERGY

Several years ago I was fortunate to attend a seminar conducted by the Pacific Coast Institute. Though the topic was not urgency, the principle of synergy that was addressed offered a practical and powerful method of conveying urgency.

Consider that a mule is capable of pulling a load of approximately eight-thousand pounds. Therefore, it would seem reasonable to assume two mules could manage sixteen thousand pounds. In actuality, two mules that have been trained to pull together can far exceed sixteen thousand pounds and easily handle eighteen to twenty thousand pounds.

So how does this relate to sales? The application is this: If the entire sales team works in unison to create a sense of urgency, the effect will be greater.

Keep in mind that with adult learning, it takes six repetitions to attain a retention level of 62 percent. This means a key point during your presentation must be repeated six times before your prospect mentally absorbs it. Therefore, it is imperative that, when conveying urgency to your prospects, they hear over and over again urgency-building facts from the salesperson with whom they are working as well as the *entire team*. Every team member should work with one another to synergistically amplify urgency in the sales center, model homes, and out on the property. Team members passing one another with their prospects in tow should convey facts overheard by the prospects and deciphered as urgent. Here's an example:

Superachiever: "Bill, before you take your guest to the models or out to the property, I'm happy to say we've had another family join our community. Home (or homesite) 142 is now sold and you should remove this fine property from your list of available homes (or homesites.)"

URGENCY SURROUNDS YOU

Here are some ways to create a sense of urgency.

❑ **ONE-OF-A-KIND:** The most common, yet powerful form of urgency is the "one-of-a-kind." People will buy almost anything that they perceive to be one-of-a-kind. The beauty of real estate is that, because of the uniqueness of every home, condominium, townhome or patio home, it truly a one-of-a-kind.

In discussing the fact that the property is one-of-a-kind, it is important that you take the initiative to control inventory. Even if you have 75 homesites, you cannot possibly show that many at one time. You only sell one at a time, so you should first determine which ones you will be showing.

Obviously, the first person to make a decision on a home or homesite should be the salesperson. If you have not decided in advance the limited properties to show and demonstrate to each customer, your prospect will not be able to make a decision either. The choice must be narrowed down to two or three, and then to one as quickly as possible. Failure to do this gives your prospect time to "think it over" and possibly decide not to own at all.

INCREASE IN PROPERTY VALUES: A pricing strategy should be designed to assist sales momentum. By scheduling price adjustments in advance, developers and builders can give their sales team a good presentation point that causes immediate urgency. Increases in prices are normally structured within predevelopment or preconstruction stages and give early investors an advantage.

Prescheduled price increases can only be achieved with the controlled release of inventory during phases of development. This avoids over-supply, and allows the opportunity to increase prices as sales occur, which stimulates buyers to act today rather than experience higher prices tomorrow. Also, it will increase the values of homes and homesites already purchased. This gives you happy owners, who sometimes can earn a return on investment prior to closing. But more importantly, by controlling inventory to enhance values, a clear message is sent to buyers that the longer they procrastinate, the more it costs them later.

 POSSESSION DATES AND SCHEDULING: Move-in and possession is almost always part of the consideration in a decision to own a new home. If construction time is 90 to 120 days, and the closing of their resale home is within the same time frame, then the meter of urgency is ticking. With second homes and vacation homes, possession and delivery can be of paramount importance if the home is to be completed "in season" for personal use or if rental income is important, especially if it is factored into the loan to qualify the prospect.

 PRODUCTION SCHEDULES: A missed opportunity to create urgency is found in the selection process that goes with the acquisition of a new home. When additional features—or even customary features such as carpet, appliances, and wall coverings—need to be selected, this presents you with an opportunity to move prospects ahead in the decision-making process. At a critical point in the sales conversation, you might say something to the effect of:

Superachiever: "Mr. and Mrs. Prospect, I can appreciate your needing a little more time to think it over, but we are at a critical point in construction. Wall covering, carpet selection and tiles must be selected *now*. You still have the opportunity to have your *brand new home* customized exclusively for you rather than having to settle for our decorator's taste."

☐ **SELLING FROM STRENGTH:** With urgency, it is important to sell from a position of strength, to appear indifferent about whether the prospect buys or doesn't buy. In our teenage years, we called this playing hard-to-get with respect to getting dates.

Selling from strength uses the element of reverse psychology that makes people want something they may not be able to get. In other words, you create a need (desire for gain) and then indicate it may be hard to fulfill (fear of loss).

THE TAKE-AWAY CLOSE

This is the preferred closing strategy when conveying urgency. You must possess and convey an "I don't care" attitude and be able to sell from strength. The point is, you really do not care if the prospect becomes involved, because regardless if she chooses to own or not, someone else is waiting to seize the opportunity to purchase a home from you.

This close is rooted in the prospect's "fear of loss." Although you have been encouraging a "desire for gain" by giving a brilliant presentation, the prospects may be hesitating and indecisive. So, rather than continue to speak in terms of what the prospects gain, you shift gears and now speak in terms of what the prospects will lose by not taking action.

Superachiever: "Mr. and Mrs. Prospect, I can see you are absolutely enthralled with this gorgeous home/homesite. But, since you are unable to make up your mind, I have a suggestion that will help you avoid disappointment. As you are aware, this is the only home/homesite at this price/location, etc. In the event someone else decides to purchase your home/homesite before you do, why don't we go select another one, *almost as nice?*"

The critical instruction: **Remain perfectly silent!**

Prospect: "We don't want a homesite *almost* as nice."

Superachiever: "I understand. The initial investment is only $___. Will you be using cash or personal check today?"

Prospect: *The strategies may not work 100 percent of the time.* For instance, they may respond with, "We'll take our chances," or "If it's meant to be, it's meant to be."

Superachiever: "What! Are you sure that if someone were to take *your* homesite, that would be okay, and you are willing to settle for second best? Mr. and Mrs. Prospect, you just don't seem like the type of people who would settle for second best, are you?"

Prospect: They may now respond with, "This is really pushing," or "We are just not comfortable."

Superachiever: "I understand. It's just that, in the past, so many people just like you have come back after a few days only to discover their homesites are now owned by someone else. I just don't want that to happen to you."

In summary, attitude, confident expectations, enthusiasm, and fear are emotions that convey and maintain a sense of urgency. Your role is to get the prospect emotionally charged. Also, it is important that your entire sales team maintain a positive synergy with urgency that contagiously spreads among prospects as they enter your sales center or model homes. Your entire demeanor and presentation should suggest that you work in a community where customers are beating down your doors for the opportunity to own in your neighborhood.

Okay. Enough preplanning. As they say in the military, "Let's take the hill ...now!"

6

STEP 1 OF THE POWER PROCESS: MEET AND GREET

People spend money when and where they feel good.
~ Walt Disney

We sell new homes — (so) make them feel at home.
~ Nicki Joy

∾ঔ৾   ∾ঔ৾   ∾ঔ৾

Perhaps the most misunderstood aspect of new home and neighborhood sales is how to meet and greet your guests (prospects) professionally as they enter your showcase homes and sales centers.

Keep in mind that first impressions are lasting impressions and you will never get a second chance to make a good *first impression*. So, begin with the realization that the first few seconds of exposure to your sales center, and to you, are critical to a great first impression.

THE DEADLY SIN: PREJUDGING

Adhere to this adage throughout your selling career: "Prejudging is not prequalifying." Many salespeople try to determine the customer's ability and willingness to own by prejudging. Prejudging usually occurs during the initial moments of the meeting. The salesperson may judge the customer by his or her appearance, car or job.

During a sales meeting, Steve, a top producer, explained how his father, a successful surgeon, shops for high-ticket merchandise such as luxury automobiles and real estate investments. He never reveals his profession and also intentionally dresses down, driving his older car to appear less than qualified. Steve's father has been able to shop unattended and almost inconspicuously. If he drove his Jaguar and dressed in his professional attire, he most likely would receive a lot of attention.

It is human nature that makes our first impressions our lasting impressions, but you must resist and not judge people superficially. Ability and willingness to own are not determined by outward appearances. Consider the advice of Henry Ward Beecher: "When you want to know the worth of a man, count what is in him, not on him."

Just as you can't judge this book by its cover, you can't judge people by their coverings. Neither this book nor people will give you any insights if you don't take the time to read them.

Even though it is in our nature to prejudge during our first few moments of the initial contact with the prospect, remember the prospect will also prejudge you. It is important that you portray a professional image of yourself, your product, and your company. Although you don't want to stand out and be conspicuous, you still can be *part* of the crowd without being *lost* in the crowd. By packaging and presenting yourself the best way you can, you show you care about yourself; and when you care, others will. When meeting and greeting prospects, be energetic, enthusiastic and efficient; look poised, polished, and prepared.

The second time prejudging of the prospect may occur is during the presentation when a salesperson decides the prospect does not want to own because she asks too many questions or voices concerns or objections. The salesperson loses heart.

Remember, a sale is a transfer of emotions. The moment you decide the prospect will not own is when your energy and enthusiasm dissipate and you deliver a poor presentation.

A few points to consider about the prospects as they enter your sales center and home:

1. **Most of your prospects are probably confused.** Psychologists tell us all persons are uneasy when entering a strange surround-

ing, such as a sales center, and they lack confidence in meeting a salesperson the first time.

You must also realize a new home or homesite isn't a disposable item and is not purchased on a daily basis. When you consider people will purchase a new home only a few times in their lives, at the most, you realize they truly are not experienced shoppers. That's why they need you. You've done their homework for them. You are in a position to advise them, consult with them, and make them feel comfortable and "at home" *before* they buy their homes.

2. **Most of your prospects are in a hurry.** As mentioned before, your competition is aggressively chasing your prospect and the statistics clearly indicate that you may expect the potential buyer to visit multiple communities. Remember that homebuyers are shopping by the process of exclusion. And, when shopping by the process of elimination, they are in a hurry to cross you off their shopping lists. Therefore, it's even more important that you make a habit of performing at a consistently higher level than your competition.

3. **Your prospect may enter your sales center with a hardened approach.** Numerous homebuyers believe a hardened approach is their first safeguard to buying. Many times a truly serious purchaser may assume the role of "reluctant buyer" and immediately greet you with the predictable, "I'm just looking."

I'M JUST LOOKING

We need to discuss this response. There are two power points to remember about anyone who enters a buying situation and says, "I'm just looking."

First, for the most part, no one enters a sales center or showcase home "just to look." Remember, a new home/homesite is a major purchase that occurs only a few times in a customer's life. Therefore, your prospects really aren't just looking, but on a mission to own.

Second, it is the greeting you use that will cause the homebuyer to reflexively respond, "I'm just looking."

Imagine yourself in a buying situation. Have you ever entered a store or showroom, literally on a mission to buy, and a salesperson approaches you with, "May I help you?" What's your reply going to be? That's right. "No thanks, just looking."

"Just looking" is the natural, ingrained response. To illustrate, let me share with you an actual case study that was performed by one of our country's major retail department store chains.

The study was conducted by having regular store personnel greet customers who approached the counter with, "May I help you?" They found that the closing ratio was two out of ten who were converted to a buyer.

Next, using the same product with a control group behind the counter, the greeting was changed to a similar one that will be given to you on page 64 and here's what they found: "May I help you?" resulted in a closed sales ratio of 2 out of 10, whereas the similar greeting, which you will be taught, resulted in a closed sales ratio of 6 out of 10. That's amazing. A 20 percent closing ratio jumps to a 60 percent ratio!

If you discovered a new way of meeting and greeting your prospects that would guarantee a significant increase in your sales, would you use it? Most of you are thinking, "Sure! I'd use it." But the reality is (referring to the chapter on change) you may have already developed the habit of greeting with "May I help you?" so your natural tendency will be to avoid leaving your comfort zone to try something new.

Or course, it bears repeating that the definition of insanity is doing the same thing over and over and expecting a different result each time.

If you are a new salesperson, a new greeting will not pose a challenge to you. But if you are a veteran salesperson, be prepared for some discomfort as you try to change.

Why do I mention this? Because psychologists tell us it takes 21 days to develop a new habit. This is important to know because, if you only try this new greeting once or twice, or even six or eight times, and it doesn't work immediately, or you're the least bit uncomfortable, you may quit too soon and revert to your old standby, "May I help you?"

Let's look at that new way of greeting and meeting your guests as they enter your showcase homes and sales centers.

THE PROCESS OF GREETING BEGINS WITH THE FIRST FEW SECONDS

Experts agree that judgment is being passed in the first one to four seconds that a prospect and salesperson meet and the judgment is finalized and complete within the first 30 seconds. If your prospects' first glance is favorable, you may expect them to act and respond positively during your sale's conversation. However, if your prospects' first impression formulates a negative opinion, they will respond adversely.

So, instead of asking a prospect "May I help you?" use the following upbeat greeting and approach:

- ❑ **Exercise a warm professional approach:** "Hi, it's a great day, isn't it?"

- ❑ **Give your name to get their name:** "My name is ___, and yours is?"

- ❑ **Extend a handshake:** At the same time you give your name, extend your hand, maintain eye contact and offer a firm handshake.

- ❑ **Welcome them to the community:** "Thank you for visiting ___. Please make yourself at home."

SAMPLE SCRIPT

Superachiever: "Hi, it's a great day, isn't it? My name is ___; yours is? Thank you for visiting ____. Please make yourself at home."

Immediately transition to:

Superachiever: "Looking at new homes is a lot of fun, isn't it?"

The prospect's only reply will be "yes" or "no."

The Prospect Replies "Yes"

Superachiever: "Looking at new homes is a lot of fun, isn't it?"

Prospect: "Yes."

Superachiever: "Outstanding! What type/kind of home are you looking for?"

Prospect: (Allow them to elaborate.)

Superachiever: "Mr. and Mrs. Prospect, about how much time do you have to look at our community/homes/homesites?"

> NOTE: *Your strategy is to get them to commit to a definite amount of time and slow them down.*

Prospect: "We have a few minutes" or "We're in a hurry" or "We're on our way to (the store, airport, etc.)."

Superachiever: "Well, in that amount of time, I'll make sure you receive whatever literature you desire and that you see our homes/homesites/community. But first, let me take a moment to give you a quick overview of (community), its location, our amenities, and our homes/homesites, okay?"

The Prospect Replies "No"

Superachiever: "Looking at new homes is a lot of fun, isn't it?"

Prospect: "No." (No means that they are tired and frustrated with shopping and are nearing the end of their buying process).

Superachiever: "You sound frustrated."

Prospect: (Allow them to elaborate)

Superachiever: "I can certainly understand your frustration, so I promise to make shopping for a brand new home fun for you at (community). By the way, about how much time do you have to look at our community/homes/homesites?"

> NOTE: *Your strategy is to get them to commit to a definite amount of time and to slow them down.*

Prospect: "We have ____ minutes" or "We're on our way to ____." or "We're in a hurry."

Superachiever: "Well, in that amount of time, I'll make sure you receive whatever literature you desire and that you see our homes/homesites/community. But first, let me take a moment to give you a quick overview of (community), its location, our amenities, and our homes/homesites, okay?"

THE PROSPECT'S OPENING MANEUVERS

No strategy (greeting) will work 100 percent of the time. Therefore, you must have at your disposal fallback scripts and dialogs. Remember that the prospect is in a hurry, overwhelmed and of the belief that a hardened approach is the first safeguard to buying.

The following responses are opening maneuvers the prospect may employ.

> NOTE: *Your tactics to counter the prospect's opening maneuvers are known as speed bumps. A speed bump is a question that is designed to slow the prospect down and help you regain control.*

❑ *Do you have a brochure and/or price list?*

Superachiever: "Certainly. I would like to customize a brochure just for you. Please come in, tell me exactly what you are looking for, and

I'll put together your information and have you back on the road in two to three minutes."

> NOTE: *People* shop *by brochures, but* buy *by looking. It has been suggested that 75 percent of all brochures end up in the trash within 24 to 72 hours.*

☐ *We only have a few minutes.*

Superachiever: "I understand. Many of my best customers, who became happy owners, said exactly the same thing. Since you are in a hurry, let me give you a quick overview to save you valuable time."

OR

Superachiever: "I understand and, since you only have a few minutes, I'll make sure you receive some literature and visit our models and I will have you back on the road quickly. Let me take just a moment and give you a quick overview of the location of our community, our amenities and the lifestyle our community will offer you and your family."

☐ *We have just started shopping.*

Superachiever: "Outstanding! Then you have come to the right neighborhood first. I can equip you with good information, show you our amenities and homes, and then you can use (community) as the standard of measurement while you evaluate the other communities you'll shop. That's just smart business, isn't it?"

☐ *My spouse is staying in the car.*

Superachiever: "Let's walk out to the car and give your husband/wife/family a quick 60 second overview and perhaps we can prompt them to come in."

☐ *Do you have a price list?*

Superachiever: "Mr. and Mrs. Prospect, I'm excited to assemble an advertising package for you; however, I will not be including a price list. May I explain why? As shown on our plat map, the red flags indicate sold properties. As a matter of fact, our rate of sale is __ new homes/homesites per week. The reason we do not include a price list is because, whatever is available today will, in all probability, be gone tomorrow. Also, as rapidly as properties are moving, we never know when to expect a price increase. What I'm going to include in your package are the price ranges you desire, and then I'll call you periodically with the status of sold properties and price increases."

> NOTE: *The psychology of followup is that the prospect must have a reason to come back/call back and the salesperson must have a reason to call back/invite back. It is vital to understand the strategy of withholding information. If you give the critical information, such as a price sheet, the prospect no longer needs your assistance and has no reason to come back to your sales center/model home. Additionally, you will destroy the sense of urgency by showing all the availability's that appear on a price sheet.*

ADDITIONAL GREETINGS

■ **Multiple groups.**

When there are several prospective buyers at a time, then greet all the individual prospects with a "congregational" greeting. You are attempting to discover who in the group is a genuine prospect.

Superachiever: "Hi, welcome to ___. My name is ___. As you can see, we are always busy at ___. Why don't you gather around and I'll give you a brief group presentation and assemble literature for those who may be interested? Oh, by the way, who is interested in owning a new home/homesite?"

■ **Agency disclosure.**

My personal opinion aside, "agency disclosure" is mandatory. Your entire strategy is complying with the requirements of the law without complicating the process.

Superachiever: "Hi, it's a great day, isn't it? Welcome to ___. My name is ___ and you are?"

"Before giving you a brief overview, I represent the builder/developer. Are you familiar with the state of ___ agency disclosure form?"

■ **The separating couple.**

Remember, in most cases, it takes both the husband and wife, or "significant other," to render a decision. Many times at the beginning or during your presentation, a couple may separate. Initially you must keep them together to give them both a quick overview, at least to start them in the right direction, before they begin shopping by the process of exclusion.

Superachiever: "Mary, John, if just for the first few minutes you would both stick with me, I'm going to give you a quick overview of our community as well as the amenities and the floor plans our builders offer. After that, please make yourself at home and look in any direction you would like to go at your leisure. But for now, stay with me please."

■ **Realtor does all the talking.**

Do a "be honest." The cooperating broker has good reason to be defensive. It's his or her customer, so she or he has every right to desire maintaining control.

Superachiever: "Welcome to ___. My name is ___, and yours is?" (Realtors will either verbally identify themselves or hand you their cards.)

"Thank you, Mrs. Realtor, it's good to meet you, and your customer's name is? Welcome Mr. and Mrs. Customer. You are very lucky to be with Mrs. Realtor. By reputation she is one of the finest professionals in the area, and you are fortunate to have someone as knowledgeable to assist you."

"I'm sure you both are in a hurry, so I'll make certain you receive a brochure and see our models at your leisure. However, I'd like to take just a moment and give you a brief overview about our location, amenities, and homes/homesites."

OR

Superachiever: Compliment the realtor in front of the prospect and say: "Mrs. Realtor is an expert on the general area of our town, and I'm the resident expert on the specifics of this community. Together, I'm sure Mrs. Realtor and I can provide you with all the important information you will need to make an informed decision."

> NOTE: *Abraham Lincoln's strategy for winning a debate was to determine the issues of the counter-parties in advance. From there he would develop his questions and answers and then present the case from their points of view.*

7

STEP 2 OF THE POWER PROCESS: DISCOVERY
Your Key to Quota Busting

Keep away from people who try to belittle your ambitions. Small people always do that, but the really great make you feel that you too, can become great.

~ Mark Twain

Fear is that little darkroom where negatives are developed.

~ Anonymous

❧   ❧   ❧

Your goal in professional selling is to determine each home-buyer's needs and financial ability, offer solutions and conclude the transaction as soon as possible. However, before you are able to lead your potential customer through the Power Process from presentation to close, it is essential to qualify the prospect.

If you are tempted to ignore the critical step of qualifying, keep in mind that the sale initiates with the buyer who can make the decision. Therefore, investing time with qualified prospects is your key to high sales volume. In fact, sales research reflects that as many as two-thirds of today's presentations by salespeople are wasted on individuals who are not qualified to purchase. Considering this, is it surprising that sales can be so frustrating at times?

As logical and sensible as it seems to enter the process of discovery and of qualifying prospects, most salespeople still fail to do so, and immediately launch into their presentation, focusing on the assumed needs of the customer. As a result, the nonprofessional salesperson who does not qualify his prospects ends up demoralized and disheartened, unable to understand why he is having a difficult time closing his sales.

The fact is you simply cannot conclude a sale in your neighborhood with an unqualified individual or family. Your may complete the paperwork, but you won't complete the sale. Your prospect must like the new home/homesite, your community, its location, as well as have the money, desire, credit history, and authority to purchase.

Consequently, your first priority and continuing mission throughout the Power Process should always be to align yourself with those persons who are qualified.

WHY SHOULD YOU GO THROUGH THE PROCESS OF DISCOVERY?

- **Discovery determines wants, needs and desires.** Today, homebuyers feel most community salespeople are insensitive and uncaring. They mistakenly believe a community salesperson's top priority is simply making the sale. Period. They do not feel that you, as their salesperson, truly care about providing the right home for their unique needs.

Qualification is a process of discovery, and discovery helps both you and the prospects. A major part of your job is to uncover their true agenda, emotional and otherwise, and to focus on *true reality*, not the prospects' (or your) *perception* of reality.

- **Discovery provides you with the prospect's financial status.** Once you determine if their needs can be satisfied by your community and the area in which it is located, your next priority is to discover whether the prospect has the financial ability to take advantage of your homesites and homes. If financial resources are not adequate, then truly there is no reason to waste their time or yours.

By asking the right questions and not forming a hasty conclusion based upon their appearance, you discover where your prospect stands financially.

In the bestseller *The Millionaire Next Door*, the authors profiled today's millionaires, revealing that "they live well below their means. They don't drive flashy cars, and they dress conservatively. They allocate their time, energy and money efficiently in ways conducive to building wealth and believe financial independence is more important than displaying high social status." The bottom line is: What you see isn't always what you get.

- **Discovery provides you with the prospect's financial parameters.** Never oversell or undersell the potential customer. You qualify based on what is affordable and will accommodate the need. Only present and demonstrate homes and homesites within the financial parameters that best meet the needs of your prospects.

If you present a $40,000 interior homesite to a $150,000 golf fairway customer, you will frustrate the prospect and probably lose the sale. Conversely, if you present a half-million-dollar home to a customer whose financial ability is a quarter of a million, you risk alienating the prospect and losing the sale.

- **Discovery determines which parties are involved in the decision to own.** There is nothing more frustrating than to knock someone's socks off with a dynamic presentation, have the transaction mentally and emotionally wrapped up, only to find out that the sale is contingent upon someone else, such as a spouse, partner, parent, child or friend. If all parties are not available, then realize you may first be giving an overview, and then rescheduling your presentation for a time that better suits everyone's needs.

- **Discovery determines time frame.** It is essential that you know *when* the prospect is willing or able to take advantage

73

of your offer. Determine whether he wants to purchase today, next week, a month or a year from now.

■ **Discovery reveals your competition.** When you are qualifying, you may learn about the other neighborhoods and builders who are competing for the same customer. It allows you to structure your presentation with your competitors, amenities, homes, and prices in mind.

■ **Discovery helps eliminate objections before they appear.** If you question skillfully and listen attentively, prospective purchasers will tell you everything you need to know to help them with their home-buying decision. Ask the right discovery questions and allow the prospect the opportunity to talk about herself and her concerns. Then listen. Aside from the information you receive, you will also be able to determine if she is preoccupied, impatient, disinterested or indifferent.

In a book written many years ago by Barbara Walters entitled *How to Talk With Anybody About Practically Anything*, she offers this timeless advice: Regardless of whom you approach, don't think it's hopeless to attempt a conversation. Wade in and anticipate an interesting time. But be prepared to listen. The barriers between people aren't caused by a failure to talk to one another but by a failure to listen.

CONTROLLING THE FEAR OF DISCOVERY

Even though the process of discovery is very important, most salespeople avoid it. Why? Beyond fearing the process of discovery itself, the average salesperson perceives he or she will be viewed as an intruder, probing into the prospect's personal territory, which encompasses their wants, needs, desires, financial resources, and authority to purchase. The reality is you cannot help potential homebuyers with the most significant emotional and financial decision of their lives until you fully understand their needs and financial status.

The discovery part of the Power Process is simply a sharing of knowledge. In essence, you are saying to the prospect, "I know all about the community and these new homes and homesites. You know all about you. When we combine this information, we will have enough knowledge on which to make a solid decision that will be in your best interest. Now, you go first. Then I will be better equipped to match my property with your preferences."

THE ISSUE OF CONTROL

If you have problems controlling the sales process and influencing people positively in their best interests, you probably have problems with being a community salesperson as well.

In nearly every meeting of two or more people, there is a dominant person who controls the sales conversation. When you're with a prospect, that person should be *you*.

You have to be in control in order to lead the prospect through the sales process. The only way you can lead is to control the process (not the customer) with your scripts and dialogs.

So *forget* your fear of asking the discovery questions. Instead, *focus* on the rewards of having a satisfied customer and a successful career.

THE FIVE CATEGORIES OF DISCOVERY

There are five basic categories of discovery that you must investigate before you begin your sales presentation, the demonstration of your community and homes, and to conclude the sale.

1. **AREA**

   The number-one consideration your prospect will have while shopping for a home in a new neighborhood is **the area**. Regardless of how dazzling your presentation is and how glorious your community and its homes are, customers will not own in a geographic area that does not fit their values and emotional agenda.

   Think for a moment. If someone were to ask directions to your home, your reply most likely wouldn't start with a street address. Normally, you give your county or city first, then your neighborhood and finally your street address.

When selling new homes, you must sell from the *outside in*. The average salesperson sells from the *inside out*. They rush the homebuyer out to their homes and homesites first, then talk briefly about the community, with no regard as to discovering why the prospect wants to be in the particular geographic range where the neighborhood and homes are located. Allow me to illustrate this. After viewing your homes, have you ever had a potential customer say, "I wish this home were in another community" or "We love the neighborhood, but we are too far from work, school districts, shopping, facilities, etc."?

Outside-in selling has the salesperson comprehending that people don't just live in homes. They live in a particular area, within the confines of the neighborhood in which their homes are located. Consider the following:

❑ For year-round communities, the distance to work, school districts, a church or synagogue, medical facilities, and shopping areas is the top priority in the prospect's mind.

❑ In resort/retirement communities, the challenge may magnify. You must first determine if your state is right for them, and their preference for the mountains, the coast, or being inland. Also, keep in mind, for resort/retirement communities, the **hottest prospects** are those who have previously visited and/or continuously visit your area. The repeat visitor is already sold on the location.

2. **TIME FRAME**
How urgent is the need? How soon can the appropriate person take advantage of your offering? The time frame is critical. It determines the sales presentation, urgency and follow-up procedures, when you can close the sale, and when you will be paid.

You will find time frame and financial resources normally will coincide with one another. In other words, if a prospect says he is 90 days, six months, or a year from purchasing, you will find there is a condition—such as selling his home—that prohibits the immediate sale.

3. **FINANCIAL RESOURCES (MONEY)**

This is a crucial category. Your prospects may want or need your offering, but if your neighborhood and homes are not within their financial parameters, start searching for a qualified prospect.

It is important during this phase to be able to differentiate between wants and needs. By nature we always want more than we need.

I've represented luxury second homes in oceanfront and golf course communities. Interior homes, without an ocean or fairway view, sold from $450,000 up. Oceanfront homes ranged in price from $800,000 to more than a million dollars. Without fail, everyone who viewed the property chose to own the oceanfront or fairway properties. My sales team and I understood that, although everyone wanted the premier properties, only a select few could afford them. The majority of our sales were interior homes because of their affordability. Even though most buyers may want oceanfront or fairway property, if they can't afford it, then their decision to buy must be based upon what they need, not upon what they want. This is true in any new home sales offering.

Also, a new homesite or home will usually require bank financing, so you may need to qualify your prospect in two separate categories.

☐ **Down payment or initial investment:** To borrow money, you must have money. When financial terms are offered, banks or financial institutions may require the customer to have a position of equity. They want the buyers to be "at risk" with them.

☐ **Monthly payment or monthly investment:** Your prospect must qualify with her ability to afford the monthly investment. Reputable banks require a customer to meet specific debt ratios in proportion to income. In other words, banks will only allow a certain amount of debt to be incurred by the customer.

4. **AUTHORITY**

Determining who will be responsible for the purchase decision is vitally important. Will you be able to follow up, secure and deliver your presentation to all persons involved in the decision to purchase? Don't delude yourself. In the case of a couple buying a home, there are always two people involved in the decision—both husband and wife or both partners.

Keep in mind that the couple is shopping by the "process of exclusion," and today it is common for one person to first visit communities alone in order to cross them off the list. After locating the perfect neighborhood and homes, the other partner will then appear to look over the ones that have been pre-screened and selected. So, attempting to close the sale without both decision-makers present will usually result in no decision, or a delayed decision to own.

In resort real estate, I have been involved with partnerships, joint ventures, and syndicates that purchased investment properties as a group. In most cases, I met first with one individual who assured me he was the decision-maker, representing the interest of the entire group. In the early days of my career, I was gullible and believed this was true, so I would give presentations and attempt to conclude the transaction with this individual instead of the entire group. I quickly learned all partners pertinent to the decision to own must be present when a group of investors is involved. One of the greatest errors a salesperson can make is to believe the prospect who says, "I make all the decisions. Just tell me what you have to offer."

5. **WANTS, NEEDS AND DESIRES**

Qualifying has an intimidating, even judgmental tone associated to it. Nevertheless, your entire goal, through the process of discovery, is to get to know your customers before showing homes and homesites in order that they might assess your neighborhood in terms of how it will satisfy their living standards.

The key to discovery is not information dumping. It's information gathering. Of course, discovery will not occur at one specific moment. It reveals itself as your relationship with the customer develops.

Rapid-fire qualifying may be necessary in high-traffic neighborhoods. But, for the most part, your discovery questions should be conversational and not confrontational. Otherwise, you risk transferring to the customer the impression that you are trying to determine if they are worthy of your time.

When you ask questions, it helps you:

- ☐ Understand your prospect better.

- ☐ Lock in on the prospect's needs and how they relate to a new home or homesite.

- ☐ Know why it's important to meet those needs.

- ☐ Establish a relationship with the prospect by practicing the law of reciprocity—a mutual exchange of information.

- ☐ Create a more professional image by being a more informed salesperson.

- ☐ Determine the prospect's buying power.

- ☐ Recognize who all the decision-makers are.

- ☐ Learn about your prospect's passions and motivations in purchasing a new home.

- ☐ Place the prospect at ease. Remember your prospects are uncomfortable when they walk in the front door of your sales center or model home. They are in unfamiliar territory. By engaging them in relaxed conversation, you can ease their anxiety.

Your entire purpose is to question their needs, and then create your presentation around those needs. However, if you deliver a solid presentation and the prospective buyer has no desire for your neighborhood, its location and homes, or he lacks financial resources, then simply cut your presentation short, exit gracefully and press on to the next opportunity.

DISCOVERY SCRIPTS

Discovering the Area for Year-round Homes

Superachiever: "Bill, Mary, let me give you a brief overview of our community. As you see by our map, we are located (geographically). You will notice we are only ___ miles from the school district, a few minutes from the area's best shopping and churches/synagogues, and medical facilities."

A. "Oh, by the way, look at this aerial photograph. Where are you presently living?"

B. "Why are you considering moving to the area?" and/or "Why are you considering a new home? Is it the school district? Is it the shopping? Is it convenient to work? Is it to move out of/into the city?"

> NOTE: *From your area map, progress to your community map and establish a connection between your property and what the prospect needs. In doing this, a good rule of thumb is to begin by showing the home in its largest context. You help your customers visualize the neighborhood in the city, the home in the neighborhood, the rooms in the home, and their furniture in the rooms.*

As demonstrated below, you should also use your community map to give the prospect a sense of urgency.

Superachiever: "Mr. and Mrs. Prospect, before discussing our amenities, you will notice on our community map some homesites are tagged/flagged in red. These indicate the homesites that have already been sold. As you can see, we are quite busy at (community). As a matter of fact, we have ___ homes/homesites that are purchased daily/weekly by families/people just like you." (You may consider pausing for a response, or continue with:)

Superachiever: "Mr. and Mrs. Prospect, you are going to love (community). As you can see by the number of homes/homesites that have been sold, people love our homes/community. We tell all our customers it's not *if* you will fall in love with our community/homes/homesite, but *when*. Will we still have what you are looking for, considering how fast the property is selling? Will we be able to have your new home built as soon as you need it?"

Discovering the Area for Resort/Retirement Communities

Prospect: "We are just beginning to drive the coast."

Superachiever: "Bill, Mary, let me give you a brief overview of our community. As you can see by looking at our aerial map, we are located in (state). In driving the coast, you will have several states to select. **A)** Have you narrowed your choice of states? **B)** Have you decided whether you would prefer mountains, inland, or coast?"

> NOTE: *Your best prospects are those who have either visited or vacationed in your specific state/county/town. This means the first sale (area) is made. If they are unfamiliar with your area, you must make two sales. First, sell your area and, second, your community.*
>
> *From your aerial map showing the states, you would then progress to your town map, locating your medical facilities, shopping, etc. From the town map, you would progress to your community map to create urgency and present your community's amenities.*

Discovering the Time Frame

As mentioned earlier, you must determine through discovery if there is a reason your prospects cannot buy their homes immediately.

Superachiever: "Ms. Prospect, how soon have you thought of making a move?" or "How soon before you invest in your new home/homesite?" or "How soon before you plan on moving into your new home?"

Prospect: "Probably six months."

Superachiever: "Really! What will be different then?"

Prospect: "I'll have sold my home."

> NOTE: *On the surface she seems to be unqualified. Continue to probe.*

Superachiever: "I'm curious. Is it that you *need* to sell your home or that you would just feel more comfortable if you sold your home first?"

Prospect: "I would just feel more comfortable."

> NOTE: *By probing you may have taken what initially seemed an UNqualified prospect and helped her realize her own qualifications. Keep probing.*

Superachiever: "I guess what I'm asking is, if you found the perfect property at the ideal price, would it be necessary to wait until your home sells, or would you take advantage of the right opportunity if it came along today?"

Prospect: "If it were the right opportunity, I guess I could move."

> NOTE: *By probing, you have taken what initially seemed an UNqualified prospect and proven to yourself and to her that her time frame may not disqualify her from purchasing now.*

In the event a prospect says he must sell his home first, you proceed with the following script:

Superachiever: "Mr. Prospect, I'm curious. Is it that you must sell your home or would you just feel more comfortable if you sold your home first?"

Prospect: "No, I have to sell my home."

> NOTE: *Probe and further qualify the situation.*

Superachiever: "I understand. Have you listed your home?"

> NOTE: *If they answer "No," they are too far into the future. Focus on a qualified prospect. If they have listed their home ask:*

Superachiever: "Great, how's the market?" or, for the prospect who is renting, "How soon before your lease expires?"

    ஃ   ஃ   ஃ

Superachiever: "I'm curious, how long have you been looking at new communities/new homes?"

Prospect: "This week." or "Six months." or "Three years."

Superachiever: "What communities/homes have you looked at? What did you like best about _____? What did you like least? What kept you from investing? or What are you still looking for?"

    ஃ   ஃ   ஃ

Superachiever: "Mr. Prospect, there are only two considerations in regards to real estate and your investment time frame. The two considerations are price and availability. First, you can feel certain that whatever is available today will probably be gone tomorrow. Second, in all probability the values will increase. I'm wondering, have *you* noticed increasing values and diminishing availability in your shopping process?"

Discovering the Financial Resources

When qualifying financial resources, buyers often start with a pre-conceived notion of how much they would *like* to invest, versus how much they will *actually* invest. In other words, *willingness to pay* and *ability to pay* are two separate issues. New homebuyers initially shop *logically*, but they buy *emotionally* and seldom do they stay within their budgets. Try this script to determine the true investment range by employing the two words "up to."

Superachiever: "Mr. and Mrs. prospect, what investment range are you considering with your new home/homesite?"

Prospect: "About $180,000."

Superachiever: Respond quickly and curiously with: "up to."

Prospect: "Maybe $200,000 to $250,000." (If your prospects change their investment position, then you have learned the true investment range.)

> NOTE: *The prospects may not change their investment range and may respond by saying something to the effect:*

Prospect: "There is no 'up to.' We've settled at $180,000 period."

Superachiever: "I understand. At the same time, not wanting to perform a disservice to you, if there were a particular home/homesite that was $5,000 to $10,000 more than your investment range, should I show this to you, or is $180,000 your absolute ceiling?"

Superachiever: "Mr. and Mrs. Prospect, our homes range from $___ to $___ and would require an initial investment of only $___. Have you set that amount aside or made arrangements for the initial investment?"

Superachiever: "Congratulations on the sale of your home/homesite. How much of what you realized from the sale will you be rolling over to your new home/homesite?"

Superachiever: "Miss Prospect, have you secured your financial arrangements or would you like me to handle the details for you?"

✻   ✻   ✻

Superachiever: "Mr. Prospect, have you been to your bank yet?"

Prospect: "No."

Superachiever: "Could I make a suggestion? We have wonderful relationships with many outstanding financial institutions. As a matter of fact, let's make an appointment now, regardless if this is the community of your choice. At least this way, you will know exactly where you stand."

> NOTE: *Securing the appointment has several advantages. 1) It allows you to sell a home prior to their bank visit, on a contingency basis; 2) It assures the continuing appointment; 3) It temporarily takes them out of the market by forming a business relationship with you.*

Discovering Wants, Needs, and Desires

Your strategy is to help them determine their hot buttons so, when you progress to the demonstration/site selection portion of the sales process, you show only properties that satisfy their emotional agendas as well as their financial parameters.

Superachiever: "Mr. and Mrs. Prospect, have you specifically decided on a particular floor plan? What I'm really asking is, do you know how many bedrooms and baths you want?

Prospect: The customers may respond "yes." If so, ask them to describe their new home. However, the prospect may respond by saying, "We don't know." or "We're just out getting ideas." Regardless of the response...

Superachiever: "What type of home do you have now?" Lead them to tell you about the features, number of bedrooms, kitchen, baths, dining room, yard, etc. (Being creatures of habit, you will often discover they want many of the same features again.)

Superachiever: "Your home sounds wonderful. May I ask if there is anything about your home that you would change or improve?"

> *Note: You should have arrived at their true hot button.*

Qualifying a Noncommitted Buyer

Many times you will have visitors who are "just looking" and are curious to see model homes or their decor. Do not discount this prospect. Countless homes have been purchased by those who are "just looking." Once a spectacular design or amenity-filled community has bred discontent, a great salesperson can help the now dissatisfied homeowners own the home of their dreams.

Superachiever: "Mr. and Mrs. Prospect, how long have you lived in your present home?" Regardless of the answer, follow up by saying: "I'm sure it was a great investment. I'm curious though, knowing what you know now, is there anything you would change about your home?"

Prospect: Allow them to elaborate.

Superachiever: "How about your neighborhood? Has it changed and developed the way you originally anticipated?"

> NOTE: *Allow them to elaborate and if they express discontent with what they have now, you are in a position to proceed with your presentation.*

Superachiever: "Mr. and Mrs. Prospect, that's why so many people just like you are relocating to (community). Let me give you a quick overview and you will discover for yourself why everyone wants to live in _____."

Discovering the Decision-Makers (Authority)

Your goal is to quickly determine who the decision-makers are. This creates a challenge because of nontraditional relationships, so you must delicately discover who will be living in the home.

❧   ❧   ❧

Superachiever: "Ms. Prospect, how many people will be enjoying your new home?"

Prospect: "Four."

Superachiever: "Outstanding, and that would be?"

Prospect: "My two children and significant other."

Superachiever: "How many bedrooms will you require?"

Prospect: "Four, I guess."

Superachiever: "Your bedroom plus two for the children equals three bedrooms. I'm curious, how would you use the fourth room—as a home office, den or guestroom?"

Prospect: "As a home office."

Superachiever: "Ms. Prospect, we have two phenomenal homes/ floor plans that include four bedrooms. Let's go take a look. Oh, by the way, when can we assemble everyone together to take a look at your new home?"

First-Time Homebuyers

Frequently, first-time homebuyers will have a "phantom buyer" (parent, relative, friend) in the background. This strategy works well if the phantom buyer is a Realtor or any other expert advising them.

❧   ❧   ❧

Superachiever: "You are fortunate to have someone so knowledgeable help you with your selection process. Let's set up a convenient time to meet around both of your schedules so he can experience first hand why you are so excited about the opportunities at (community)."

> NOTE: *When you secure the appointment, realize the advisor will play a critical role in the final decision. Regardless of how much time you have invested with your prospect, you must start back at the beginning and go through the entire sales process with the advisor.*

Partners in Real Estate

This strategy is primarily for resort real estate. But beware. Normally when a partner, such as a relative or a friend, is necessary, it's a sure sign of a financially unqualified prospect.

Your strategy is to determine the qualification of one buyer independent of the other.

✿ ✿ ✿

Superachiever: "Bill, Mary, I'm curious, if Jan and Mike were unable or not interested in owning this property after you two view it, would you be in a position to proceed forward?"

Bill and Mary: "Yes."

OR

Superachiever: "Jan and Mike, if Bill and Mary were not interested in owning this property, would you proceed forward?"

Jan and Mike: "I'm not sure." or "No."

> NOTE: *You know if Jan and Mike fall in love with the property and Bill and Mary do not, you do not stand a chance of selling it. Conversely, if Jan and Mike do not like the property, then Bill and Mary are still viable prospects. If this is the case, you may consider separating the two couples, since many times the disinterested or*

unqualified prospect can negate the interested party's decision in their justification process.

BECOME A REJECTION SPECIALIST

Discovery is a process that will continue through the course of the entire sales process. But many questions will need to be answered as you and the prospect decide whether or not you will enter into a business relationship. You must ask the questions in advance to conclude if this is a qualified candidate.

Changing your perception about rejection: At the beginning of this chapter, I pointed out that experts now agree that as many as two-thirds of today's sales presentations are being delivered to nonqualified buyers. With this thought in mind, here are two questions:

❑ Now that you are aware of the five categories of discovery, have you previously been guilty of giving presentations to nonqualified buyers?

❑ Can you have an abundance of appointments and be successful?

Think carefully before you reply. If you have been in sales for any period of time, you have probably heard that sales is a numbers game and that the secret is, if you put yourself in front of enough people, a certain number will purchase.

As already mentioned, this is not necessarily true. You can have unlimited traffic and still not be successful, especially if your conversations are with those who are not qualified to take advantage of your offering.

What will change your perception about rejection, and cause you to become unbelievably excited about sales in general? As a salesperson, you experience rejection not because you fail to present or demonstrate, but because of your failure to qualify through the process of discovery.

Salespeople often cause their own anxiety and discouragement by failing to qualify the prospect. Once you commit to the discovery process, you should be the one to decide whether or not to continue forward with a particular individual or couple.

Most salespeople see the potential customer as the person in the driver's seat, with the power to either reject or accept the salesperson and the offer. They actually view the individual(s) with whom they are working as the rejecter, and see themselves as the *rejectees*.

From this day on, restructure your thinking and see yourself, the discoverer, as the rejecter and your unqualified leads and prospects as the rejectees. **You** become the person in charge of pushing the reject button.

Turn the tables on rejection by qualifying your buyers. Prospects have to jump through these five hoops before you invest your time with them:

1. Area

2. Time frame

3. Authority

4. Wants, needs and desires

5. Financial ability

If they cannot get through enough of the hoops—graciously reject them and move on to a qualified prospect. Your closings will occur almost naturally when you devote your time and energy to the right people.

A DOCTOR OF SALES

Doctors always diagnosis before they prescribe. Prescription prior to diagnosis would be malpractice. As a salesperson, you must also diagnose (determine the condition of your prospect) before you prescribe (offer a remedy). Presentation before qualification is malpractice. Invest 10 to 30 minutes of your time in discovery first, and eliminate wasting hours, days, or possibly months delivering presentations and attempting to close sales with those who cannot, or will not, purchase from you.

ONE FINAL THOUGHT

There are signposts along the road of life. When one has deceived you, do you lengthen your stride or look for a place to sit down?

Sometimes a prospect will deceive you. When this happens, do you become discouraged and want to sit the next one out, or do you try harder to find the truth the next time around? Adversity of any kind can break you or cause you to break records. You can't control everything that happens to you, but you can control your reactions.

8

STEP 3 OF THE POWER PROCESS: PRESENTATION/OVERVIEW
Retrofitting Your Sales Center to the Power Process

You now have to decide what "images" you want for your brand. Image means personality. Products, like people, have personalities, which can make or break them in the marketplace.
~ **Advertising mogul David Ogilvy**

If you don't get noticed, you don't have anything. You just have to be noticed, but the art is in getting noticed naturally, without screaming or without tricks.
~ **Advertising writer Leo Burnett**

❧   ❧   ❧

T he absolute best place to sell a new homesite or home (whether it is a villa, a private residence, or a townhome) is in its actual location. The marketing practice of on-site sales begins by inviting the prospect to your specific sales center or model home(s) to demonstrate the lifestyle of your community and advantages of your new homes.

The on-site sales and information center should be a focal point of the sales process. Regardless of whether your sales center is a trailer, a converted garage, a model home or an elaborate office, the objective of on-site marketing is to provide an emotionally-charged environment that prepares the prospect for an organized overview and presentation of what you have to offer.

Every sales office should convey a sense of arrival and have a comfortable place to greet and quickly qualify buyers as the salesperson introduces the community and housing designs. The first three steps of the sales process (meet and greet, discovery, presentation and overview) require special props and sales exhibits organized and displayed in a very specific order.

There are two major points that must be understood in designing a sales center and exhibits when working the power process.

First, understand that Step 2 (Discovery) and Step 3 (Presentation and Overview) **are simultaneous events**. In other words, discovery and presentation for the most part occur "conversationally" and are a function of the sales center and exhibits.

Second, the exhibits at the sales center are the tools the salesperson needs in order to control traffic, to qualify the buyer, to create urgency and to deliver a brief presentation prior to the prospective buyer going to the property and viewing the homes.

The proper ingredients of a sales center are discussed in the subsequent paragraphs. Each exhibit should be presented in the order listed.

INGREDIENT 1: THE LOCATION MAP

As specified in Chapter 2, "Discovery," the location or geographic range of your community will always be the top consideration in the homebuyer's mind. The most effective area map is an aerial photograph showing the location of your community in relation to nearby cities and towns. It should identify medical facilities, shopping centers, churches, schools and any other conveniences that would be influencing factors and a concern for the prospect. It is always best to place the area map immediately at the entrance of the sales center. This has a two-fold benefit. First, it allows the salesperson to show the prospects where they currently live in relation to the community's location. Second, it allows the salesperson to describe area attractions to the prospects. Refer back to pages 80-81 (Chapter 7, Discovery) and review how to skillfully point out how your location meets your prospect's unique set of living requirements.

INGREDIENT 2: PLOT MAP OF THE COMMUNITY

This map is easily the most important exhibit in the sales center, and a vital tool to the salesperson. Two different maps or displays are required for maximum effectiveness. One is an overall wall plot map of the community, or a relief map on a site table that shows the entire neighborhood with all amenities, villages and expansion phases. You use this map or site table to orient your prospect to the entire community concept. If appropriate, discuss amenities such as pools, tennis courts, a golf course, security gates, fitness centers, and biking/walking/jogging trails. This gives you the chance to begin setting the stage for the lifestyle your prospects will enjoy individually or as a family. The map is not to identify specific lot lines but to give an overview of the neighborhood's lifestyle. Showing future unsold phases with lot lines indicates too much availability and completely diminishes a sense of urgency.

With urgency in mind, the second plot map is by far the most commanding visual aid. Unlike the overall community map, this particular map identifies the specific area or phase of development where current sales are occurring. The key to this map is to flag all sold properties with red sold labels. Refer back to the script on page 81, and you can create an immediate sense of urgency by showing your tagged map and by quoting your company's rate of sales.

INGREDIENT 3: LIFESTYLE WALL

Neighborhood sales is an emotional business. The adage, "A picture is worth a thousand words," is personified with the marketing of a new home and neighborhood. Quoting facts and figures is the logical portion of your presentation, but to convince your prospects that your neighborhood offers the social lifestyle they seek requires pictures of people in real-life situations. A picture of a pool, the tennis courts, fitness center, golf course, or even a landscape without the faces of people enjoying themselves is devoid of social activity. You need to use imagery to get your customers thinking in pictures. When you can't show them something, use descriptive words. Make your customers feel that the community, the neighborhood, and the home is theirs. Cultivate their ability to picture themselves swimming,

95

playing tennis, working out, golfing or gardening. Touch their hearts and you get them emotionally involved.

One of the most effective displays includes pictures of owners and their new homes. Add testimonial letters and endorsements to the pictures and you will visually reinforce, "We have happy owners, just like you, who have already made the "smart choice." If there is not enough wall space to convey the lifestyle, then include a photo album that can be shown during the sales presentation.

The Sequence of Events

You have presented the area and discovered why they are considering moving. At this juncture, it would be appropriate to ask the prospect a trial-closing question.

Superachiever: "Mr. and Mrs. Prospect, can you imagine yourself living in city or county (area)?" or "Does the city or county (area) meet your requirements in regards to distance to your work, school district and available medical and shopping facilities?" This is an important question, because in the event the prospects were to answer "no" to the area, your presentation has virtually ended.

How can your presentation be over if it hasn't even included having the prospects view the models? Acknowledge the fact that even the most glorious community, with the finest homes, will not overcome the objection and condition of a neighborhood that is not located in an area that meets the prospect's living requirements.

The problem is most salespeople do not close and gain commitment early in their overview presentation. And by failing to gain commitment, the salesperson inadvertently delivers his presentation, performs exhaustive follow up, and experiences rejection simply because he is working with a prospect who has become unqualified because of the community's location.

Let's suppose your prospects answer "yes," the area is indeed suited to their basic living requirements. Great! Now proceed to your community maps or site table to deliver the overview presentation of your neighborhood, while simultaneously creating an immediate sense of urgency by quoting your rate of sales.

INGREDIENT 4: THE BUILDER'S STORY

It bears repeating: You are selling from the "outside in." We will use the ideal scenario. Your prospects say "yes" to the area, and are excited with the general aspects and lifestyle your neighborhood offers. Now you are ready to discuss your builder/developer's credibility and possibly show some of your housing designs.

One of the functions of the properly-designed sales center and of the professional salesperson is to play up the builder/developer's credibility in presenting the greeting and overview portion of the sales process. Most often this is accomplished by graphically displaying a representative selection of homes once the prospect is qualified. However, the sales process is not as simple as just showing pictures of homes. Trust ties the process together, and it is conveyed by people. **You sell a person to a person before you attempt to sell a home to a person.** Therefore, it is important to position a picture of the builder(s) within the display of your housing lines. Let all of your prospects put faces to those they are trusting to build their dream homes.

Most builders/developers fight having their pictures displayed, wanting to keep a "low profile." And some even attempt to substantiate this low profile by saying, "Our homes speak for themselves." If this were the case, there would be no need for sales centers and professional salespeople. The point is the builders or developers who want to maintain a low profile should rethink this position and place themselves in front of today's homebuyer. A salesperson needs a builder/developer's credibility in addition to a graphic presentation of homes.

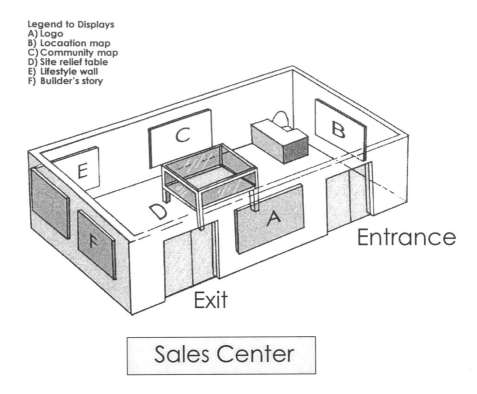

Legend to Displays
A) Logo
B) Locaation map
C) Community map
D) Site relief table
E) Lifestyle wall
F) Builder's story

Entrance

Exit

Sales Center

INGREDIENT 5: OTHER EXHIBITS

There are many other tools that can be retrofitted to the sales center or model homes. But you must carefully consider the impact each exhibit will have in terms of its ability to influence a prospect's decision to own. The following exhibits represent the most important tools.

Decorator and Color Selection Exhibits

While various options and upgrade features assist in customizing homes, they are a deterrent when discussed prior to discovery and the presentation/overview. It is best to keep such items out of the general traffic pattern, away from the central sales center. If a customer gets sidetracked in these details prior to choosing a homesite or home, she may become confused and you will lose control of the sales process. Remember, "To confuse 'em is to lose 'em." An independent room or a separate design center that is accessible after the home or homesite selection is the best place to present decorations and options.

Regarding the display of floor plans and renderings, the majority of customers cannot read floor plans and bring to life the third dimension. Floor plans displayed on the walls will impede the sales process and interrupt its proper sequence. The floor plans and renderings are best suited as a closing tool after the prospects have seen a home or selected a homesite they would want to own. Plans should be placed outside of the traffic pattern where initial discovery and qualifying occurs, and made available to a prospect only by a salesperson.

INGREDIENT 6: BROCHURES

Brochures are valuable tools only when they are used correctly and at the proper time. It seems to be the tendency of most salespeople to shove a brochure into the hands of the prospect when he first enters the sales center or model home. This very act deprives the salesperson of what she needs most, which is the opportunity to get involved with the prospect and answer his questions *after* returning from the property and models.

The solution is simple, but it causes severe withdrawal pains for many community salespeople who prefer to have brochures visible and convenient. Keep the brochures out of sight and out of the customer's hands (and mind) until the prospect finishes viewing the property and homes.

> NOTE: *In the chapter on follow up there will be an indepth discussion about the need to withhold information in order to have an effective follow-up campaign.*

INGREDIENT 7: PRICE SHEETS

Nothing kills the sense of urgency quicker than giving a prospect a price sheet that shows the availability of *everything*. Even if you have 25, 50 or 100 sites available, you do not relay that fact to the prospect. Proper qualification has you discovering *the one and only* home or homesite you will be concentrating on—based strictly on the prospect's needs, desires and financial ability.

No buyer can select from 5, much less 50. It is overwhelming. But having you do the legwork is part of demonstrating how they can trust your expertise as their new home consultant.

The choices must be narrowed to three, to two, and then to one and only one. Giving price sheets and revealing all the available property not only diminishes urgency but confuses the homebuyers. This alone may give them a reason to think it over and maybe not purchase at all. When you give the buyer brochures packed with every floor plan and price sheet, you are afflicting them with information overload. To effectively overcome the request for a price sheet refer to the script on page 66-67.

More appropriate than a price sheet would be a small plat map that has been stamped with red "sold" labels. You can then write the price ranges of the properties that specifically interest them. This allows your prospects to visually orient themselves as to where their homesites will be, while the red "sold" labels convey urgency. Remember, if you give out all the information (brochures, renderings, price sheets) the prospect has no further use of you.

A CHOREOGRAPHED PRODUCTION

As with the rest of the Power Process, your overview and presentation should be planned and rehearsed. The exhibits in the sales center should coordinate with your verbal sales presentation. Everything should work together toward one goal: inspiring the prospect to buy what he or she wants and/or needs.

In the childhood fantasy story *Alice in Wonderland*, Alice asks the Cheshire Cat, "Would you tell me please which way I ought to go from here?" The cat replied, "Well, that depends on where you want to get to."

Your prospects should never wonder, like Alice, where they want "to get to." It is your job, as their representative, to bridge the way between where they are and where they want to be. To do that, you need to be sure-footed, knowing where you stand so you won't be knocked off guard by an unanticipated question, an offhanded remark, a difficult candidate, or your competition. By memorizing scripts, coordinating your information, and following the Power Process, you can confidently face your prospects and your goals.

9

STEP 4 OF THE POWER PROCESS: DEMONSTRATION
Selling The Sizzle

Advertising puts the "wonder" in Wonder Bread.
~ Jef Richards, advertising professor/author

∽෯   ∽෯   ∽෯

One of your top competitors in new home and neighborhood sales is the prospect's own status quo. The purpose of demonstration is for you to show and sell your prospect on the idea that, "I have something better for you than what you have now."

Malcolm Forbes, a master of sales and founder of *Forbes Magazine,* observed, "In selling, your product has got to have differences that are perceived and real. You've got to fill a niche. You've got to point out the differences as a plus. You've got to have an angle, a twist, a point that differentiates you and then you've got to make the most of it."

SELL THE SIZZLE

As a young man, I was fortunate to have worked as a waiter in an upscale resort restaurant. It was here the importance of presentation and demonstration was first brought to my attention, and I later embraced it in my selling career.

In the restaurant, all broiled and grilled specialties were served on heavy metal platters. It seemed many times there was as much emphasis on heating the platter as there was on heating the food. And for good reason.

The piping hot food was quickly removed from the broiler and immediately placed on these intensely hot metal platters, which were in turn placed on large wooden serving plates. It was a phenomenal presentation. But the presentation was brought to life by the **demonstration.**

Beside the exit door of the kitchen, on the way into the dining room, was a bucket of shaved ice. Upon leaving the kitchen, the server would grab a small handful of the shaved ice and sprinkle it along the edge of the platter. The hot, metal platter on which the seafood and beef were served, had an explosive reaction with the ice and caused a popping and crackling that could be heard across the dining room.

For each waiter, it was **show time.** We sprinkled the ice on the hot platter and held the trays high as we walked to the customers. Heads would turn as we hustled through the dining room with the crackling hot food. The anticipation was rampant. We placed the platters in front of each customer, along with this instruction: "Be careful. The food and platter are extremely hot. This dish was just prepared exclusively for you."

This illustration teaches a solid lesson about advertising. The sale was not the food; **the sale was the sizzle.** Perception becomes reality and perception is made real by sizzling demonstrations. The perception was that a hot, sizzling steak was being delivered. The reality was that the sizzling had nothing to do with the steak. Nevertheless, before the customers even tasted the steaks, the presentation was making their mouths water. The pleasure caused by the demonstration of the sizzle was so overwhelming that satisfaction with the food (product) was almost guaranteed.

The restaurant analysis directly relates to community sales. Your customers do not necessarily buy the tangible values (sticks and bricks) of your neighborhood and homes. They first buy the feelings or perceptions of gratification that your neighborhood and homes will satisfy. They are craving that sizzle that will make their mouths water.

Your customers choose to own in a community setting for emotional reasons, and in doing so, they must perceive an enhancement of their personal and/or family's lifestyle. Therefore, the demonstration of your neighborhood amenities, homes and homesites is the most powerful part of the sales process.

To help you lock-in on the significance of this concept, let me point out that the word "community" is derived from the word "communication." The community traditionally has been a place where people gather and discuss life, problems and common interests. It's where families group together to enjoy planned activities, good conversation, and each other's company. This is one of the benefits of shared amenities such as tennis courts, swimming pools, playgrounds, and picnic areas.

Today, many buyers are looking for this sense of belonging. Others, including the economically stable Baby Boomers, are looking to recapture feelings from their youth. They are old enough to remember pleasant evenings of neighborhood "stoop sitting." Before homes had air conditioning, residents would sit on the porch stoop, or stairs, to cool off on hot days. Frequently, they would be joined by their neighbors and, over a glass of iced tea, would solve the problems of the world. They would sit and talk until the mosquitoes or the late hour forced them inside.

Recently, a friend of mind was reminiscing about being a newly-wed living in a row house in Baltimore. His eyes had a far-away look as he recalled many happy days strolling down the sidewalk, hand-in-hand with his bride, heading for the neighborhood park where they would listen to birds chirping, children playing, and friends talking. On the way, they would stop to visit with neighbors who were outside working in their yards, walking their dogs, or pushing strollers. He turned to me and said wishfully, "Boy! I wish I could find that again."

The truth is, of course, we can't go back in time, but we can reconnect with those feelings. And it is your job, as a professional salesperson, to make those feelings "sizzle"—to make them come alive again by demonstrating that in your community, the perception can become the reality.

DIFFERENTIAL DEMONSTRATION

Superachievers sell the **differentials**—the diversity separating their communities from the vast array of offerings available to the consumer.

If you have been in real estate or community sales for any amount of time, you have probably heard the adage, "The three keys to real estate are location, location, location." Well, it's absolutely true.

Location is *the* factor that separates one neighborhood from another. Any builder/developer can, for the most part, construct homes for approximately the same cost per square foot, provided the materials in use are of the same comparable quality. But the one thing that causes values to soar is the uniqueness of one location over another.

Sixties hipster Timothy Leary once said, "Hey, if you don't like where you are, you can always pick up your needle and move to another groove." There are many people who will come into your sales center who don't like where they are. Show them the benefits of picking up and relocating to your community's "groove."

NEIGHBORHOOD AMENITIES

What is an amenity? Amenities are the outside contributions the developer builds to enhance the desirability of the community. They may start with a posh and embracing grand entryway, and then progress to a 24-hour staffed security gate adjoining an elegant clubhouse with a spectacular indoor pool and fitness center, all situated near an 18-hole championship golf course and a top-flight tennis facility.

Let's not forget the gamut of amenities may also be as simple and subtle as fiber optic lines and underground utilities, paved walkways, beautifully lit streets and exotic landscaping with an abundance of strategically-placed parks. Your mission is to be inventive in order to ingeniously demonstrate the amenities **prior** to the selection of a home or homesite. This is critical to the sales process. As location, location, location are the three keys to purchasing real estate, then the three keys to differentiating your community from others are amenities, amenities, amenities.

THE PUPPY DOG CLOSE

What do puppy dogs have to do with demonstration? Smart pet store owners sell cute little puppies by letting the prospect "give the puppy a try first."

A mother and her children walk into the pet store just to look at the puppy they see in the window. Captivated by the wiggling, adorable pup, the children begin chanting: "We want this puppy! We want this puppy!"

The pet store owner takes the dog from the display window and hands it to the mother. Immediately, the parent and children become emotionally involved with a purchase decision that they probably had not even considered before walking into the store. The children persist with, "Please Mommy, can't we have the puppy dog? We'll take care of it. Can't we take it home with us, PLEASE!?"

The store owner senses her apprehension and then issues the Puppy Dog Close.

"This is a major decision, so why don't you just give it a try? We have a one-week return policy. Take the puppy home for a few days and play with him! If you don't feel comfortable, just bring him back."

The parent reluctantly agrees, thinking it's no obligation to just "give it a try" and bring it back in a couple of days after the kids discover they really don't want the responsibility of a dog.

However, what usually happens is that the puppy takes on an identity and is given a name. He looks up at everyone with those soft brown eyes, and cuddles in each family member's lap. The kids are enamored. The parents are smitten. Suddenly, that cute little puppy dog is part of the family and the sale is consummated.

A powerful demonstration, wouldn't you agree? Some of the most successful neighborhoods in the world are using this type of strategy. Of course, they don't allow you to physically take the "home" home, but they do take you out on the property, allow you to experience it and get emotionally involved, and then take this emotional remnant home with you.

It's applying the "Try it. You'll like it," philosophy. And it works. The concept is even taught to children. In fact, an entire book was written around this one premise. Dr. Seuss' *Green Eggs and Ham* has a storyline in which the persistent Sam-I-am tries to get his friend to taste green eggs and ham, a food he has never tried before but is certain he does not like. After emphatically claiming that he would not like them in the rain, on a train, in a box, with a fox, in a house, or with a mouse, the friend finally shouts, "I do not like them here or there. I do not like them ANYWHERE!" To which steadfast Sam replies, "You do not like them. So you say. Try them! Try them! And you may." You probably know what happens. He tries them and, to his surprise, he likes green eggs and ham. Sam was a good salesman.

To drive the point home, a sale is emotional and, to pique emotional responses, you must let the prospect see, touch, feel, smell and hear the benefits of living in your neighborhood. Involve the senses and you involve emotions. Whether someone's selling puppy dogs or green eggs and ham, if it's new, it is necessary to have the customer experience the product so the feeling of ownership is internalized. It is imperative that you demonstrate your amenities — that you "sell the sizzle."

HOME DEMONSTRATION

"Outside-in selling" has you starting with the area, then presenting the community, and finally focusing on the demonstration of your homes and homesites.

The importance of the new home demonstration cannot be over emphasized. Too often potential customers will hurriedly run through a home. Their unaided, casual inspection causes them to miss the subtleties and ingredients that make your home designs unique.

It takes the demonstration of the onsite sales professional to effectively assist a discriminating buyer. As a specialist in new home and neighborhood sales, you must be prepared to justify and demonstrate the values in a manner that accentuates the positive benefits of your distinctive homes.

HOT BUTTON CLOSE

The Hot Button Close is founded on the 80/20 rule: 80 percent of all results come from 20 percent of energy expended. In sales, we say the top 20 percent of the sales team makes 80 percent of the sales. The other 20 percent of the sales volume is shared by the remaining 80 percent of the sales force. Because this is the irrefutable case in all sales organizations, I always advise people in management to maximize results by investing 80 percent of their time with the top 20 percent of the sales team.

The 80/20 rule in selling products or services is based on the fact that 80 percent of the buying decisions will be based on 20 percent of the product's features. In other words, if your homes have ten product features and benefits, your job is to find the one or two features that represent key benefits to the person buying your product, and push his or her hot button repeatedly.

Anita Roddick understood the importance of identifying a single "hot button" when she established the Body Shop, a worldwide franchise of stores that focuses on personal care. She assumed that other people in the world shared her concern about finding healthy ways of caring for themselves that would not adversely affect the environment.

In his book *The Roaring 2000s: How to Achieve Personal and Financial Success in the Greatest Boom in History,* author Harry Dent writes, "Roddick assumed that people would be moved by the impact of such natural consumption habits on the benefits to traditional industries of third world countries and the resultant preservation of rain forests. ...She understood and invested in one of the most fundamental trends of the new generation: environmental and health concerns."

"The best entrepreneurs, executives and investors I have worked with who actually achieve the highest returns and build the most wealth, despite often being involved in (change), don't perceive that they are taking big risks at all. They are simply doing the obvious. They are very definite about what they are doing. ...They have a clear understanding of change and fundamental trends."

Trends are our collective "hot buttons." When enough of us respond to issues or items that pique our interest, such as an environmentally sensitive company producing personal care products, we unknowingly start a trend.

All of us have emotional areas of sensitivity. Your job, as a salesperson, is to find those areas that will ignite your prospects' enthusiasm and pique their interest.

THE BEAUTIFUL, FLOWERING CHERRY TREE: AN EXAMPLE OF HOT-BUTTON SELLING

A real estate professional shows an older home to a couple. The home is in need of some repair. Upon arriving they see a beautiful flowering cherry tree in the front yard. The wife, who seems to be the more dominant one, says to her husband, "Look, Tom, a beautiful flowering cherry tree. When I was a young girl, my family home had a beautiful cherry tree, and I've always dreamed our home would have a tree just like this one."

Tom nudges his wife and says, "Let me handle this. I'll do the talking."

The salesperson identifies the hot button, makes a mental note and prepares the presentation.

Tom is playing reluctant buyer and says, "The deck needs immediate repair." The salesperson agrees, "Yes, but from your deck, you would always enjoy the view of the beautiful flowering cherry tree." They go through the house and Tom says, "The carpet needs to be replaced and the house needs to be painted." The salesperson replies, "You're right, but from the bay window you have a glorious view of the beautiful flowering cherry tree." Upon viewing the master bed-

110

room, Tom objects, "The bedroom is small and the bathrooms need new fixtures." "Yes, but from here you have a perfect view of the beautiful flowering cherry tree."

At the end of the showing, Mrs. Prospect, who loves the beautiful flowering cherry tree, convinces her husband to buy the home.

The cherry tree was the hot button, the emotional key that was pushed over and over until the decision was rendered. If you question skillfully and listen intently, the buyers will tell you exactly what will make them purchase a home or homesite in your neighborhood. Not only will they tell you what will cause them to own, but also what would cause them not to own.

Pay strict attention to their buying signals, determine the key benefits, and build your sales presentation around the hot buttons.

THE KEY TO DEMONSTRATION

The challenge with demonstration is facing the reality. Prospects first come to your community to get a sense of the neighborhood, to view the models, to determine your prices, but *not* to meet a salesperson. This fact is simple: Prospects believe the least amount of contact they have with a salesperson, the better off they will be. Your battle is uphill and you must persuade them quickly that you are an intricate part of their shopping process and it's in their best interests that you accompany them.

One thing all experts agree upon and top sales professionals substantiate is the belief that demonstration is where the elite salesperson sets himself or herself apart from the competition and gains a noticeable selling advantage. The power of demonstration is so persuasive to a prospect that you will never reach your full potential if you do not utilize this tool.

FOLLOW ME

It has been said that the number-one mistake with onsite sales is failure to ask for the order. This undoubtedly is true; however, for now let's review what is probably the second biggest mistake.

The number-two mistake is failure to bridge or transition to the demonstration with your **"follow me attitude."** You never ask permission. You lead boldly and confidently.

When interviewing top producers, they all say going from the sales center to the property and models is merely a natural event. They simply say to their prospects, "Let's go," and then lead them out the door. It's that easy!

Yet for most salespeople, this "follow me" attitude is one of the most difficult parts of the process. Revisit chapter five; specifically, the section on fear. First, overcome your fear of asking. Second, remember "no" is just a knee-jerk reaction, a natural response. Therefore, it is of paramount importance that you do not ask, "Do you mind if I show you the models?" or "If you have just a few minutes, could I show you our community?" Given the choice between having you escort them to the models or going unattended, they will most likely request a brochure and price list, and then forge ahead alone.

You do not have to have an apologetic attitude, or feel you are bothering a prospect. Nevertheless, some salespeople actually delude themselves with the belief that prospects will be annoyed if they do their job and go with them.

The point is you are not *suggesting* you would like to go with them on the property or to the models. You are initiating an "assumptive approach." If you assume (believe) it's in their best interests for you to accompany them, you will approach the demonstration enthusiastically and boldly, saying to them, "Follow me, let's go!"

THE DEMONSTRATION IS ALWAYS FROM YOUR CAR

Many times a buyer will insist on following you in his or her own car. This is discouraged because it is impossible to demonstrate your community and deliver your presentation in separate automobiles. Remember your "follow me attitude."

Prospect: "We'll follow you in our car."

Superachiever: "Mr. and Mrs. Prospect, it's important that you ride with me. We have many exciting features and amenities with our community that your family will miss unless I personally show you. Come on, let's all go in my car."

Prospect: "No, really, we will just follow you."

Superachiever: "That's okay, I'll ride with you." (Walk directly to their car and get in.)

> NOTE: *We assume, if they are not golfers, we do not have to show the course; or if they are not boaters, we do not have to show the marina; or if they are out of shape, we do not show the fitness center. The opposite is true. When selling to the emotions, you are a dream merchant. Paint them a mental picture of themselves as members of the boating community, or swapping stories in the clubhouse after their first round of golf, or being soothed in the sauna at the end of a stressful workday. With your guidance, they can visualize the lifestyle they dream of having.*

✦   ✦   ✦

THE PROSPECT WANTS TO VIEW THE MODELS UNATTENDED

Superachiever: "Mr. Prospect, I can sense you would prefer to look at the models by yourself, and I want you to feel free to do so at your leisure. At the same time, if it would be okay with you, I'd like to quickly show you the first model and give you a brief preview of the unique custom features we build into all our homes. That's okay with you, isn't it?" **Remember your "follow me attitude."**

✦   ✦   ✦

THE PROSPECT WANTS A PLAT AND PRICE SHEET TO VIEW HOMESITES UNATTENDED

Superachiever: "Ms. Prospect, a lot of times people want to view the homesites themselves first, but without fail they come back confused and frustrated. Though our homesites are numbered, identifying the property lines can sometimes be a challenge. Also, you will need someone to give you a quick overview of the community's features and amenities. I only have a few minutes myself. Why don't I take you out, get you started and once you are familiar with the neighborhood, I can come back to the office? That makes sense, doesn't it?"

> NOTE: *If the prospect is obstinate, continuously requesting a brochure and insistent upon viewing the property without your assistance, proceed with:*

Superachiever: "Mr. and Mrs. Prospect, I'm excited to assemble some information for you; however, I will not be including a price list. May I explain why? As shown on our plat map, the red flags indicate sold properties. As a matter of fact, our rate of sale is __ new homes/new homesites per week. The reason we do not include a price list is because whatever is available today will in all probability be gone tomorrow. Also, as rapidly as properties are moving, we never know when to expect a price increase. What I'm going to include with your information are the price ranges you desire, and then I'll call you periodically with the status of sold properties and price increases. That's okay with you, isn't it?"

> NOTE: *The psychology of follow up is that the prospect must have a reason to come back/call back and the salesperson must have a reason to call back/invite back. It is vital to understand the strategy of withholding information. If you give the critical information, such as a price sheet, the prospect no longer needs your assistance and has no reason to come back to your sales center/model home. Remember the process of exclusion. The prospect is looking for a reason to cross you off his list.*

THE PROSPECT QUESTIONS THE TYPES
OF NEIGHBORS WHO LIVE IN THE COMMUNITY

It is a violation of federal, state, local government and civil rights enforcement groups to answer specific questions concerning race, religion, and sexual or familial status. You must not violate the law while also remaining diplomatic and cheerful.

Prospect: "What kinds of people (or what types of people) make up the neighborhood?"

Superachiever: "Your neighbors are people just like you, and everyone is a satisfied customer."

> NOTE: *If the prospect persists or becomes specific, respond with:*

Superachiever: "Mr. and Mrs. Prospect, according to federal law, no one selling real estate is allowed to discuss the ethnic, racial or age groups of a neighborhood. I'm sure you understand my position."

> NOTE: *Brush the issue aside and continue forward. However, if they persist, your only choice would be to answer:*

Superachiever: "Mr. and Mrs. Prospect, I'm curious: Are you a member of any federal, state, local government agency, or civil rights group?" If they are members, they must offer disclosure. This should end the inquiry.

To help make the sale, you must "sell the sizzle"— the perception of what's "hot" in your community—along with the real bricks and mortar. To do this, you should creatively and professionally demonstrate your new homes and community. And to demonstrate them, you must *personally* accompany the prospect. It's an interlocking process.

This approach will also help you maintain a visual impact with the prospect. Position yourself and package your information so that the prospect senses your presence, even when you aren't around. When he sees what you're selling, he should be seeing (or sensing) you.

In closing, here's a final example of "selling the sizzle." Most of us recognize the name Bill Gates. *People* magazine reported, "He is to software what Thomas Edison was to light bulbs."

The future founder of Microsoft became involved with computers and business while in seventh grade at a private school in Seattle. One summer he earned more than $4,000 programming the school schedules on a timeshare mainframe. Then Gates and his school buddy, Paul Allen, founded a small company called Traf-O-Data, which used a new Intel microprocessor to analyze traffic patterns in Seattle. In its first year of business, the company grossed $20,000. Bill Gates was 15 years old.

At 17, Gates took a formal leave of absence from school and he and Allen were hired by TRW to develop software at a reported salary of $30,000. He later returned to school and attended Harvard, only to drop out to start his own company, Microsoft. It became the top software company in the world, making him the world's youngest billionaire at the ripe old age of 30.

What does any of this have to do with "selling the sizzle?" Well, between Traf-O-Data and TRW, when he was 16, Gates went to Congress as a page and witnessed, up close, the 1972 Nixon verses McGovern campaign. His entrepreneurial spirit surfaced, and he bought 5,000 Democratic campaign buttons expecting to profit from the forthcoming campaign. Unfortunately, after he bought the buttons, McGovern dumped his running mate, Senator Eagleton. Gates suddenly found that he had paid five cents each for campaign buttons that were now obsolete.

So what did he do? He sold the "sizzle." Repositioning himself, he refocused, not on reality, but on what buyers might perceive reality to be. He discovered an angle that was "hot," and began marketing the campaign buttons as historical and rare memorabilia. He sold every one of them, some at $25 each.

10

STEP 5 OF THE POWER PROCESS: HOME/HOMESITE SELECTIONS
The "One and Only One"

Always remember you're unique ...just like everyone else.
~ Bumper sticker

❧   ❧   ❧

After demonstrating the community to the prospect, you are now in a position to choose a home or a homesite. In this step, you actually take your prospects to the tangible location(s) available for selection. Or you take them to completed homes that are ready for their instantaneous ownership.

If you have models, it's best to progress to your showcase homes first where everything is complete. This way, the prospect can carry a vision of a finished, and possibly furnished, home to the homesites you plan to show. Additionally, when showing an unimproved homesite, you now benefit by having mental pictures working for you.

TO BUILD OR NOT TO BUILD

The case for models is a never-ending debate, but it can be simplified with the realization that people buy what they can observe and experience. Model home selling provides a comfortable, warm environment, and a more congenial and casual atmosphere.

As important as models are to the selection process, so is the merchandising of the home. New home/neighborhood sales have entered the retail arena. Merchandising is of paramount importance.

In fact, the November 1997 issue of *Builder Magazine* published the results of a homebuyer's survey, which asked, "Did the interior furnishing and decorating play an important part in deciding which model to buy?" You bet it did! A resounding 54 percent responded: "Yes, furnishings and decorating helped visualize how a home can best be lived in."

SQUARE FOOTAGE

To maximize the value of your homes, point out the total square footage, including decks, porches, garage, basement, etc. Only after giving the total square footage state the specific living area.

Superachiever: "Mr. Prospect, this particular showcase home is ___ft. (state total square footage including decks, garage, etc.) with ___ft. that's actual living area. The garage, decks and basement comprise the additional space."

    ✑   ✑   ✑

UNFINISHED MODELS

When showing unmerchandised or undecorated homes, many times they will not rise to the customer's expectations as well as a furnished home.

Superachiever: "Mr. and Mrs. Prospect, the home you are going to see will not be furnished or have any accessorized items. We do this intentionally so, as you view the home, you will be able to visualize how *you* might decorate it."

> NOTE: *When you show your customers the empty rooms, give them time to hang their thoughts there. Allow them the freedom to use their imagination by not interrupting their thinking.*

The ensuing dialogue should be used both in the unfurnished and furnished home. Following this procedure will cause them to become emotionally involved. Your prospects can only become emotionally involved by mentally picturing themselves living in the home.

❧   ❧   ❧

Dialog of the Superachiever

☑ **On the kitchen:** "Share with me, who usually cooks those great dinners in your home?" *She raises her hand.* "Great! Does your family have a favorite dish?" *She responds that they love her spaghetti sauce, which is made from a recipe passed down from her Grandmother.* "Just thinking about homemade spaghetti sauce and hot garlic bread makes my mouth water. By the way, can you imagine yourself preparing your family's favorite meals in this kitchen?" *She answers "yes." You open up the cabinets.* "Look at all this cabinet space, and the huge pantry. All this storage space would make any cook happy. Wouldn't you agree?"

❑ **On energy efficiency:** "Put your hand on this double-paned window and feel the warmth. By the way, the windows are filled with argon gas between the panes. This allows sunlight in, but filters out ultraviolet rays. The benefit is sunlight will not damage or fade your carpeting and furnishings." (If the windows tilt, then have the prospect open and close them. Or do it first to demonstrate the ease of operation, then have the prospect try it.)

☑ **On the living area:** "Tell me about your furniture. Where would you place your sofa? How would you situate your television and stereo?"

☑ **On the master suite:** "How would you place your bed? Where would you place your dresser? As you can see, we include two walk-in closets. Who would take the larger one?"

☑ **On the guest room:** "Would you use this as a guest room?" or "How could you see yourself using this room?" (Home office, exercise room, etc.)

- ❑ **On the children's room:** Conclude the sale by having the children select their rooms.

- ❑ **On the garage:** Have the husband describe how he would arrange his workshop.

- ❑ **On the yard:** "If this were your yard, how would you landscape it?"

NOTE: *Demonstrate, demonstrate, demonstrate. Selling new homes and neighborhoods is an interactive procedure in which you create the mood that causes your potential buyers to mentally move in.*

ॐ   ॐ   ॐ

SELLING WITHOUT COMPLETED HOMES

If you do not have homes that are completed and ready for occupancy, or they are on a "to-be-built basis," you must still present the benefits of having a made-to-order custom home.

Superachiever: "Ms. Prospect, our customers have proven, when given a choice between having a home built solely for them and customized to their taste, or having to settle for a home that has already been built, they much prefer taking an active role in the building process. Don't you think it would be exciting to take an active part in the most important investment of your life? You can participate in the carpet selection, counter top colors, and have your brand new home built especially for you, rather than have to settle for someone else's taste."

ॐ   ॐ   ॐ

SELECTING THE HOMESITE

From the models, you may often transport them to the homesite. Referring back to the chapter on "Discovery," the prospects' natural inclination will be to see everything you have. But unless you intentionally plan on confusing them, "everything" is entirely too much to digest. Do not show anything other than properties that are within their budgets and financial resources. If a prospect's budget is for an interior homesite, then do not show waterfront or golf course homesites. However, you may be able to satisfy a waterfront dream by showing convenient community water access. Or you may be able to satisfy a golf course mentality with a fairway view.

DEMONSTRATING HOMESITES: Establishing Uniqueness

New home sales authority Bonnie Alfried says, "Our home is our castle, but our land is our territory, and you may rest assured we are by nature territorial beings."

You sell property by not merely walking *on* it, but by walking *around* it and clearly identifying the prospect's unique "lot in life." To do so, you must be willing to clearly outline all boundaries and property lines.

To properly demonstrate a homesite requires that you have several tools in your possession. Be sure you carry a 100' tape, surveyor's Day-glo tape and the actual dimensional plat of the homesite, with the building envelope identified on the plat. Refer to Figure 10.1, and the corresponding numbers on page 122, where the process of showing a homesite is described in detail.

Figure 10.1

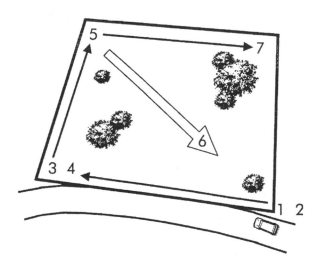

Memorize *these steps* before taking your *first step* to show the property.

❶ If driving, park your car directly in front of one of the two property pins nearest the street. Your car is now situated as an identifiable marker.

❷ Place in your prospects' hands the plat of the individual homesite. Involvement is the key. You want them talking about the dimensions of the homesite to you versus you talking about the dimensions to them.

❸ Proceed horizontally to the second property pin closest to the road.

❹ Pull out your Day-glo surveyor's tape and mark the existing property line stake, or a piece of vegetation that is immediately near the property pin. You have now clearly identified two of the four property pins.

❺ Now proceed perpendicular to the third property pin at the rear of the homesite and, with your surveyor's tape, mark the third pin.

❻ Standing by the property pin in the rear, have your prospects look diagonally in the direction of your car. The diagonal view makes even the smallest homesite appear large. Remember, perception is reality.

❼ Conclude walking the property line to the fourth and final property pin, using your surveyor's tape to mark the territory. Have your prospects again look at the property diagonally. From the fourth and final pin, all corners of the homesite are clearly indicated and you have marked their territory for their approval.

You are now ready to actually walk within the homesite's boundaries. With your 100' tape, you can determine setback lines and help them visually and physically orient their home on the homesite.

Is this procedure time consuming? Yes. But is it effective? Let me ask you a question. Would you go to closing on a homesite you were buying without a survey? For most astute investors, the answer is "no." All you are doing is surveying the homesite *in advance* for your homeowner. You will conclude more transactions using this procedure than you did in the past when you simply walked straight to the middle of the homesite without taking the time to identify the property lines.

An added benefit of this procedure is that, many times, prospects will revisit the homesite later in the day or week without you. With their territory clearly marked, they will be able to visualize their dream home on their homesite. This is another way of making your presence felt when you aren't there in person.

URGENCY AND THE HOMESITE SELECTION

How do you overcome indecision and procrastination? By creating a sense of **urgency!** You lead your prospect to take action today by convincing him that the homesite he is considering is the "one and only one." Land is unique and each property, whether 5,000 square feet or ten acres, has physical attributes that contribute to the individuality of the homesite.

Top professional salespeople emphasize the importance of owning a particular homesite by stressing the unique features of the property. Differentiate between each piece of property and prove to your customers that the homesites they have selected are each "one of a kind."

Every property you show will include one, if not several, of the following physical attributes. And remember, when showing property, quote your rate of sales because when they finally select "the one and only one," it may not be available.

 Location in the community: Is the homesite located next to the clubhouse or any special amenity? Perhaps it's situated next to a boat ramp that offers water access, or tucked directly on the green of the ninth hole.

123

Size of the homesite: You could show the largest homesite in the community, or conversely, a small, minimum-maintenance property.

 Corner homesite: Corner homesites are normally larger, and frequently offer creative placement of the home, or provide an opportunity for a circular driveway.

 Cul-de-sac: These can be preferred homesites because they are off the road, offer privacy and are safer for children. Incidentally, as land continues to become more valuable and scarce, cul-de-sacs may be eliminated because they are not deemed the best and most economically feasible use of the land.

 Exposure: Will the homesite offer sunlight, shade, breezes or natural protection from the elements?

Elevation: Is it a one-of-a-kind lot that can support panoramic views?

 Views: Unparalleled views of water, golf courses or mountains can be achieved with certain homesites, often making them a best value.

 Vegetation and trees: People will buy trees and homesites with lush natural cover and this can be especially important in areas offering no vegetation.

Green or protected areas: A homesite that backs up to a protected area may pick up additional square footage and perhaps even acreage without incurring any additional cost.

Location to other homesites: A homesite may be located next door to the most expensive home in the neighborhood, or next door to a prestigious neighbor.

THE SEQUENCE OF CLOSING QUESTIONS YOU ALWAYS ASK DURING DEMONSTRATION/SELECTION

1.   Can you picture yourself/family living in this neighborhood?

2.   Can you imagine yourself living in this home?

3.   Can you see your new home/dream home on this homesite?

❧   ❧   ❧

Superachiever: "Ms. Prospect, can you picture yourself living in this neighborhood?"

Prospect: "Yes."

Superachiever: "Great! Let's go select a home that will best meet your requirements."

Prospect: "All right."

❧   ❧   ❧

Superachiever: "Ms. Prospect, you seem excited with this particular floor plan/showcase home."

Prospect: "Yes. (or) I think so."

Superachiever: "Wonderful! Let's go select your homesite."

❧   ❧   ❧

Superachiever: "Ms. Prospect, you seem to have fallen in love with this homesite. Am I correct?"

Prospect: "It's absolutely gorgeous."

Superachiever: "It certainly is, isn't it? So can you see your new home on this homesite?"

Prospect: "Yes. (or) I think so."

Superachiever: "Outstanding! Then the next step is..."

THE NEXT STEP

Your next step is to anticipate objections. Before going further, however, let's review the first five steps of the Power Process and come to understand the importance of anticipating objections.

Step 1 of the Sales Process has you properly *meeting and greeting* in a manner that gains the prospect's confidence and trust. **Step 2** moves you into *discovery* and **Step 3** into *presentation and overview*, when you conversationally qualify and deliver an overview of the benefits of your community's location along with the attributes of the neighborhood. **Step 4** gets you into *demonstration* and to **Step 5**, which is *selection*. Here you share the unparalleled lifestyle of your neighborhood and have your prospect select the "one and only one" home or homesite. And, of course, during this entire procedure, you create urgency with the desire for gain and the fear of loss.

Now you are 80 percent there! But, because a new home or homesite represents one of the most significant emotional and financial decisions of a lifetime, you must anticipate some objections. In the next chapter, I'll show you how to handle them.

11

STEP 6 OF THE POWER PROCESS: GO AHEAD, MAKE MY DAY ...OBJECT!

My policy is to learn from the past, focus on the present, and dream about the future. I'm a firm believer in learning from adversity. Often the worst of times can turn to your advantage. My life is a study of that.

~ Donald Trump

If you find a path with no obstacles, it probably doesn't lead anywhere.

~ Businessman Frank A. Clark

ൟ   ൟ   ൟ

How can any prospect's objection to your neighborhood make your day? You may have certain notions about your prospects. You think to yourself, "My dream customer is great! We get along well, we agree, and he recognizes my community as the perfect solution to his housing needs."

Wake up and smell the Cappuccino! Many times, if your prospects do not object—do not challenge your homes and the claims you make—they will not buy either. (Refer to Chapter 5 on the fear of failure on the part of the buyer.)

Regardless of how dazzling and complete your presentation, the fear of making a mistake causes your prospects to be doubtful and hesitant, and you will have to address their concerns before you are able to conclude the sale. Problems will not go away by themselves.

They must be confronted or else they will remain as a barrier to the sale. Confronting and responding to objections helps your prospects work through these concerns and advance through the process of purchasing.

The majority of sales does not occur without objections. Even when the clients respond in an abrasive manner, they may be unconsciously telling you they are emotionally involved and interested.

❑ **Objections are questions that mean the prospect needs more information.** So what are prospects saying when they object? When he says, "I need to think it over," the prospect is actually saying, "I am not yet convinced and need additional information to be certain of the decision."

If the prospect says, "I need to talk this over with my banker, family, accountant, or any third party," she is actually saying, "I'm not yet certain. I need approval and assurances."

When the prospect says, "It's too expensive or I can get it cheaper elsewhere," he wants you to prove you offer the best value. "I do not like the terms," means "What other terms are there, or can you get me the terms I want?" And, of course, the response, "I'm just looking," during your initial contact means that they do not have enough information to make a buying decision.

❑ **Objections are your signposts.** Input from the prospect provides you with critical path markers to follow. Objections represent concerns that must be resolved during your presentation in order to close the sale. Whatever issues the prospect challenges are the most important to him and, therefore, to you. Provide the prospect with enough answers and he will own.

❑ **Objections indicate interest.** A lack of objections from your prospects also signifies a lack of interest. Normally, if they do not have the financial ability to own or have no interest, they will react to your presentation in one of two ways. They may appear unemotional, without responding to anything you say. Or they will comment "Yes, it sounds great" throughout the presentation. If the prospect responds either way, you are in trouble.

So acknowledge that, generally, no sale takes place without objections, and when you have an objection you should inwardly rejoice and say to yourself, "Thank you for making my day because you are showing an interest in my new home/neighborhood!" Your acknowledgment and decision to welcome objections enable you to overcome them instead of allowing them to overcome you. Then you can confidently move ahead and close the sale.

OBJECTIONS VERSUS CONDITIONS

There is a difference between an objection and a condition. You must understand which one you are hearing so you'll know how to respond.

An *objection* is nothing more than an unanswered question. Somewhere in your presentation you have either said something, or failed to address an issue, which leaves a question in the prospect's mind. It is fed back to you as an objection. The good thing is it's something concrete you can address and overcome.

When a prospect offers a concern (objects), you can assume it's usually prompted by at least one of three reasons:

1.   There is something not understood by the prospect.

2.   There is something the prospect does not believe.

3.   There is something the prospects are trying to cover up and you don't have all the facts.

A *condition*, on the other hand, is an obstacle. Conditions are barriers or situations that prevent a prospect from buying. For instance, a prospect says, "I cannot make a decision without my wife." That's a condition you cannot circumvent. It's a condition that says you must deliver your presentation to all decision-makers prior to moving forward with the sale.

Or the prospects may not meet the financial criteria. Perhaps they have the funds available for the initial investment but, because of past credit history, they cannot obtain a loan. Perhaps they must sell their home and cannot put adequate funds together for a year or more. In both cases, these are conditions you cannot remedy even with a brilliant presentation.

Often, you waste your time trying to conclude a sale by overcoming a condition, which means you did not prequalify or carefully listen to your prospect during the discovery phase of the process. Then, when you receive the condition, you go ballistic trying to overcome an obstacle that is immovable. Since conditions are statements of facts about your prospect, it doesn't matter how good you are, how developed your skills are, or how great your answers are. You are not going to get around a condition.

Why would you even attempt to address a condition, when all you have to do is qualify the prospect prior to beginning your presentation? If you effectively prequalify before your appointment, you will never experience a condition during your presentation. The entire purpose of discovery is to determine if there are conditions that make a sale impossible. If there are, why waste valuable time trying to overcome them? Simply suggest that the prospect return later when the conditions are eliminated.

What's interesting is that most prospects initially feel their objections are conditions. They think that, when they offer the objection, they are presenting you with an obstacle and condition of fact that prohibits them from buying. So when they say, "I can't afford it" (and you know they have the budget), you rephrase the objection in your mind to, "Show me how I can afford it." Then you can overcome the objection by offering terms. You have taken what they thought was a condition and converted it to an answerable objection.

Your job is to recognize and acknowledge two facts:

1.   If you properly prequalify during discovery and listen carefully to your prospect, you will never experience a condition as the reason for not consummating the sale.

2.   All objections are questions and requests for more information. If you answer them to the customer's satisfaction, you will close the sale.

OBJECTIONS ARE PREDICTABLE

Since the dawn of the first sales call, prospects have been telling salespeople, "I need to think it over." Or "Your homes are too expensive." Or "I need to talk to my brother's niece, whose son is in the real estate business."

The average salesperson is generally caught off guard when he or she hears, "I want to think it over." He packs up his presentation, hands the prospect a brochure, and says, "I'll give you a call after you've had time to think about it."

So, what's the good news? The good news is, since all objections are predictable, you can plan your responses in advance. Like an actor in a Broadway play, you memorize your lines (presentation) and you know the lines (objections) of the other performers (prospects). I tell people in my seminars, "You know what they are going to say in advance. Therefore, since you already know what they are going to say, your job is to know how to respond once they say it."

THE LAW OF SIX

In sales there is a universal axiom that sales trainer Brian Tracy calls *The Law of Six*. It states, "Customers really have no more than six objections to own in your neighborhood."

You may hear what seems like countless objections to sales during your career. However, if you categorize the objections you will find they normally fall into six basic categories.

In my resort real estate business, for example, the six objections are:

- location (area)
- competition
- performance (as to claims)
- finance
- third-party approval
- square-foot home pricing

After identifying all objections we regularly received, we developed ironclad scripted answers to them. Thus, once armed with airtight responses to these predictable objections, our company set new sales records.

The point is, you cannot wait until you are involved in the presentation and then try to make up an answer. You must proactively prepare in advance.

Your job as a professional is to discover for yourself, or with your sales team, the six common objections you consistently hear. Once identified, simply devise and memorize potent responses. Then, when the predictable objections surface, you can answer easily and effortlessly, and automatically move to the close.

THE CUSTOMER'S AND SALESPERSON'S OBJECTIONS

The objections you receive from the prospect are the easiest to overcome. There are also, however, the objections you, the salesperson, create in your own mind as to why a customer will not buy. And these can be the most destructive.

For example, there may be something about your community that may not make complete sense to you. Perhaps you are uneasy with the price of your homesites or the lack of amenities in your neighborhood. In any case, you are not convinced that your community is the best value available. When you deliver your presentation and the final objection is price or amenities, you happen to share the same belief as the prospect and are unable to overcome the objection. Thus, you lose the sale.

The cure for a prospect's objections requires a preplanned response. The only cure for the objections in your mind is a change of attitude!

If you find that you are silently agreeing with your prospect's objections, you must invest the time to change your attitude. Find out more about your product and support it 100 percent or begin looking for another product to sell. Negative interpretations can cripple you, while positive ones will energize you. Develop the positive mindset necessary to overcome the customer's (and your own) objections.

UNCOVER THE UNSPOKEN OBJECTION

Sometimes what prohibits the sale is the one final objection that is hidden by a series of smaller objections. Your prospect knows, if not consciously then subconsciously, that if he gives you this not-yet-spoken objection and you answer it, he will have no choice but to move forward as an owner. So he holds back this one silent objection, camouflaging it behind a smoke screen of minor objections in order to avoid the buying decision.

When you are at the point where you sense the prospect is hesitating and hiding something, ask, "Mr. Prospect, I sense a bit of hesitancy. Do you mind my asking what it is?" If you remain silent the prospect will offer an answer. Regardless of the answer, compliment the prospect with, "That's a great question. I'm glad you asked. In addition to that, is there anything else that would prohibit your proceeding forward?" Again, after you ask a closing question, the key is to be silent and allow him the opportunity to reply.

If the prospect responds, "No, that's all," then you have arrived at the final objection. If, however, the prospect offers another objection, answer that one and continue the process of asking, "In addition to that, is there anything else?" until the prospect acknowledges there are no more objections.

At this point, compliment the prospect and his final objection. "Mr. Prospect, I understand, and that makes perfect sense, so you tell me what it would take to satisfy your concerns."

Just Suppose

The *Just Suppose* method of closing is also referred to as Handling the Final Objection Close. You have led the prospect to the point where he obviously wants and needs your product, but the final objection is causing him to hesitate.

With the Just Suppose Close, you remove the final objection as the reason for not going ahead.

If the prospect says, "I'm just not sure if you can deliver my home as quickly as you say," you reply, "Mr. Prospect, I understand how you feel. *Just suppose* for a moment that I could satisfy all of your concerns in writing. Is there any other reason that would cause you not to become involved today?" At this point, he must either say no, or reveal the real reason for not proceeding forward.

This is the perfect method for blowing past a smoke-screen objection and uncovering insincere objections. By incorporating "just suppose," the prospect will either agree or lead you to another, and possibly the final, objection.

Again, remain perfectly silent and listen to his entire concern. After his answer, you may consider employing the closing technique of "subject to" or "conditional terms" selling.

With **conditional terms,** you have arrived at the final objection when the prospect says, "I need to check with my banker."

You reply, "Mr. Prospect, that makes perfect sense. Prior to speaking with your banker and to facilitate the transaction in a timely fashion, let's prepare the paperwork now, making the sale subject to your banker's final approval. This way we can start the process, and if by chance the bank does not agree with your decision, we will simply start over. That makes sense, doesn't it?"

You will never be closer to concluding the sale than at the very moment you arrive at the final objection. Instead of coming back at another time and taking a chance on the prospect's fears setting in and his emotions diminishing, ask for the order now, not later.

The **Mental Flip-Flop** is the customer's psychological justification for purchasing your product or service. The prospect makes the mental switch to that of a customer, then she psychologically enters into the process of justifying all the reasons she became an owner. Whereas, if you leave her thinking about the product as a nonowner, she does not consider all the reasons to go ahead, but instead dwells on her fears and thinks of all the reasons why she should not buy.

Always attempt to conclude the transaction at the moment you answer the final objection and take the prospect out of the market, even if it means making the sale subject to conditional terms. This way, when you return to satisfy the conditions, you are coming back to a customer who has bought instead of a prospect who has been thinking about buying.

Answer Objections in a Positive Manner

Discuss and answer all objections tactfully and delicately. As mentioned earlier, an objection is just an unanswered question in a prospect's mind. Treat the objection as a request for more information.

When you are offered an objection, remain calm, nonargumentative, and appreciative. Remember, it will be impossible to move into the closing sequence until you have answered all questions and concerns. Therefore, you want the prospect to feel free to object and to continue objecting until he's depleted all his concerns.

When you first hear an objection, be enthusiastic and grateful. "Ms. Prospect, I'm glad you brought that up." Or "Thanks for bringing that up." Then answer the objection.

Feel, Felt, Found

Another way of handling an objection is with the *Feel, Felt, Found* method. It's based on creating strong perceptions that reveal you as understanding and empathetic. It also employs the closing techniques of third-party testimonial endorsements.

For instance, the prospect says, "I can get it elsewhere for less," or "I'm not satisfied with your neighborhood location," or " We're just beginning to shop."

You respond, "Mr. Prospect, I understand how you *feel*. Many others just like you *felt* the same way initially, but once they became an owner, here is what they *found*..." Then elaborate with a third-party testimonial about someone who was in the same situation or circumstances as they are but, as a result of going ahead with the decision to purchase, experienced great success and happiness.

If the objection is price per square foot, location, service or any other concern, the phrase, "I understand how you feel," sends a strong message to the prospect that you truly care. Follow up with a third-party endorsement from the happy customer, confirming that the prospect should proceed forward.

When the prospect says it's too expensive, you can respond, "Mr. Prospect, I understand how you *feel*. I recently had a customer who was in a similar situation, and he *felt* the same as you. However, what he *found* as a result of owning was that, although the price initially seemed higher, our on-time delivery, design services and new home warranties far outweighed the value our competitor could offer."

"Tell me, is price your only concern or would reliable customer service and extended warranties also be important considerations?" Using empathy and a third-party testimonial, you can circumvent and reverse almost any objection.

More on Price Objection

You realize, of course, that you aren't the only salesperson who has ever heard an objection about price. In Zig Ziglar's book, *Secrets of Closing the Sale,* he offers the following advice when the prospect says, "It costs too much, or it's too high."

"I don't think there's any question about the price being high, Mr. Prospect, but when you add the benefits of quality, subtract the disappointments of cheapness, multiply the pleasures of buying something good, and divide the cost over a period of time, the arithmetic comes out in your favor. If it costs you a hundred dollars but does you a thousand dollars worth of good, then by any yardstick you've bought a bargain, haven't you?"

I heard the following story from a business associate. While on a trip to a trade show, he stopped at a motel for the night. The sign out front announced "Free Jacuzzi." After driving several hundred miles, this sounded appealing. When he went inside, the disinterested clerk asked him if he wanted the $40 room or the $50 room. The business-man asked him what the difference was. "Well," the clerk replied, "the $50 rooms have the free Jacuzzi."

You get what you pay for.

SIX-STEP METHOD FOR OVERCOMING OBJECTIONS

Following are the six basic steps for handling objections or addressing questions and concerns. The system was popularized by the renowned sales trainer J. Douglas Edwards. If followed, it will almost always work in your favor during the objection process.

Step 1: Hear the objection. *Use Steps*

Do not interrupt, but listen attentively to the objection entirely. Give the prospect the opportunity to express his or her emotional concerns.

You have already employed the Law of Six by identifying your six top objections and you have developed and internalized bulletproof answers. However, you must not be too quick to respond. Though you may have heard the objection one thousand times before, it is this prospect's first time expressing his or her concerns to you.

Step 2: Repeat the objection to the prospect.

This is a critical step! This strategy often helps the prospect answer his own objection as he hears it repeated to him. State the objection in a kind, nonthreatening way.

When the prospect says, "It costs too much," repeat it as a question. "It costs too much?" This method has two obvious benefits.

- ■ It makes your prospect feel important and understood.

- ■ It verifies you heard the objection.

By repeating the objection, you are in effect asking for more information.

Step 3: Question the objection.

Remember the first objections you hear may be masking a larger objection. Ask for elaboration. "Mr. Prospect, let me clarify my thinking or let me be sure I understand you correctly. If it were not for (objection), then you would proceed forward today? Is that right?" Remain silent and let him answer.

Step 4: Answer the objection with your preplanned response.

Once you're certain you have the whole story behind their concerns, you can deliver your preplanned response with confidence.

Step 5: Confirm that the objection does not block the sale.

You have answered the objection, but you now must confirm the objection is no longer a reason for the prospect to avoid becoming a buyer.

"That answers your question then, doesn't it, Mr. Prospect?" or "That makes sense to you, doesn't it?"

If the prospect is not satisfied with your answer, now is the time to know. You cannot move forward and close until you are certain the issues are satisfied. If the prospect is satisfied, move to step 6.

Step 6: Close.

It is important you understand that handling objections and the closing are events occurring simultaneously. You overcome the objection(s), then move to the close.

"Well, then, Mr. Prospect, do you have any additional questions before beginning the paperwork?"

Prospect answers, "No."

"Congratulations! I'm excited for you! By the way, John and Mary, will both your names be appearing on the agreements?"

THE FINAL WORD

In the words of the respected golfer Jack Nicholas, "It's too late to practice your game on the course, during the match."

Objections occur during the final minutes of the selling match, but that isn't the time for you to be practicing your responses. Plan ahead. Anticipate the objections, prepare your answers, internalize and memorize your replies.

To move to the rank of Superachiever, apply the three R's: **Rehearse, Review, Respond.**

Rehearse your scripts out loud. Review them in your mind. Respond promptly when you hear a prospect's objection. Do this and you will be so self-assured that objections won't be obstacles but stepping-stones.

12

STEP 7 OF THE POWER PROCESS: YOUR PROSPECT WILL REMAIN A PROSPECT UNTIL YOU CLOSE

No one wants advice, only corroboration.
~ John Steinbeck, *The Winter of Our Discontent*

A verbal contract isn't worth the paper it's written on.
~ Samuel Goldwyn

〜 〜 〜

As a salesperson, you can turn closing the sale into an exciting and positive event.

You have discovered that selling consists of greeting, discovery, presenting, demonstration, overcoming objections, and the close or natural ending to successfully meeting the homebuyer's needs.

Make no mistake—closing is the bottom line. The result is that you have a paycheck to deposit.

Before diving into the specific closing strategies and techniques, here are some valuable tips.

COMMON SELLING ERRORS

■ **Failure to ask for the order:** It's hard to believe, but the main reason people do not buy is that they are not asked to own. Up to 50 percent of all sales calls end without salespeople attempting to close even *once*.

If they do attempt to close, statistics indicate the average sale does not occur until the prospect is asked to own a minimum of five to seven times. In my estimation, five to seven attempts is a conservative guess, and I suggest that you must ask even more times using multiple closing techniques.

Only a small percentage of salespeople possess the technical ability to ask for the order multiple times. The average, not-so-successful salesperson waits until the end of the presentation, then nervously shifts back and forth, asking for the order in the following timid manner: "Is this what you had in mind?" or the classic, "Well, what do you think?"

Understand this: When you ask people what they think, you're giving them the impression that you are indecisive and their response will be, "Well, I think I want to think about it."

You must be eager, prepared and confident to close. And the more ways you know how to ask, the more likely you are to ask, and the more likely you are to close and capture that commission.

■ **Talking too much:** Most salespeople know *how* to stop talking. They just don't know *when*. There is such a thing as overselling. When it happens, it's like knocking on a turtle's shell trying to get him to stick out his head.

Mediocre, new community sales organizations focus their training on product knowledge instead of sales methods. As a result, the salesperson's presentation centers on product information and a lot of facts. Poor salespeople talk too much and want to tell everything. The prospect is not dazzled—but dazed—by a salesperson with loose lips.

The superior salesperson questions skillfully and listens attentively to the prospect's needs. She asks her way into a sale; she doesn't talk her way into it. And her words inspire, rather than tire, the buyer.

■ **Talking past the close:** The most valuable career instruction my father gave me was, "Son, when they are ready to buy, they are ready to own. Stop talking and grab your paper-work."

When you ask a closing question and your prospect confirms he is ready to own in your neighborhood, the conversation stops, your presentation ceases, and you start preparing the paperwork.

For example, you say, "The current production schedule guarantees your new home delivery by the end of August. Is that satisfactory?" Your prospect answers, "Yes, it is." At that moment, he has made the decision to own. End your presentation. Move swiftly to prepare the contractual agreements.

- **Arguing with the prospect or customer:** When you receive objections or challenges to your claims and you defend your product, you are in essence telling the customer he is wrong. People dislike being told they are wrong, even if they are. As Will Rogers stated, "Most people would learn from their mistakes if they weren't so busy denying that they made them."

You are in business to win the customer, not battle him. Always be agreeable. Remember, when people have objections, respond to them in a positive nonthreatening way. *"A man convinced against his will, is of the same opinion still."*

- **Knocking the competition:** Avoid referencing your competition. If, however, something is said about the competition—negative or positive—simply reply with, "They are a fine company, and seem to do a good job."

Bill Gove is a motivational speaker who tells the following story about a businessman named Harry, the owner of a small general-appliance store in Phoenix, Arizona. Harry was continually dealing with customers price-shopping between his store and a nearby discount appliance dealer. Harry didn't want to knock his competitor, but he was tired of losing sales and customers.

As Gove explained, "When young couples came into his store, pen and paper in hand, asking detailed questions about prices, features and model numbers, Harry was pretty sure that their next move would be to trot off to his competitor to compare price tags. After spending half an hour with a couple and patiently answering all their questions, Harry would suggest an order, and he usually got a firm, 'We want to look around at some other places.'

"His rebuttal was to nod, smile, move up close, and deliver this little speech: 'I understand that you are looking for the best deal you can find. I appreciate that because I do the same thing myself. And I know you'll probably head down to Discount Dan's and compare prices. I know I would. But after you've done that, I want you to think of one thing. When you buy from Discount Dan's, you get an appliance. A good one. I know because he sells the same appliances we do. But when you buy the same appliance here, you get one thing you can't get at Dan's. You get me. I come with the deal. I stand behind what I sell, and I want you to be happy with what you buy. That means I do everything I can to be sure you never regret doing business with me. That's a guarantee.'

"With that, Harry would wish the couple well and give them a quart of ice cream in appreciation of their interest. Now, how far away do you think that young couple is going to get, with Harry's speech ringing in their ears and a quart of vanilla ice cream in their hands, in Phoenix, in August, when it's 125 degrees in the shade?"

When to Close. How to Respond to Questions During the Close.

Donna, a new home salesperson, approached me one day after a sales meeting and said, "I'm just not sure of the exact moment, the appropriate time, to close. I've internalized and scripted my closing techniques, and I understand them. I'm just not sure of the proper moment when I should bridge to the close."

I asked, "Donna, what is your favorite part of the sales process? The greeting, discovery, presenting, demonstration, overcoming objections or closing?"

"Oh Myers, I absolutely love delivering my presentation. I'm so excited about the company, and I love showing property and homes."

"Like you, Donna, most salespeople prefer the presentation portion of the process. It is, in essence, a time for you to socialize. But what you are asking me is, when do I stop socializing and get down to business?

"What you are doing is giving the entire presentation and waiting for what you think is the one moment that is most appropriate to close. Donna, the close usually occurs at the end of the presentation, but it has been building all along throughout the presentation.

"It is the process of **gaining commitment**. You see, there are commitments and minor closes that must occur during the selling process before the prospect makes the major commitment to own.

"For example, you must first gain commitment to agree to an initial appointment, which includes a specific time and date. Donna, as insignificant as this seems, if you cannot gain the commitment and close on something as minor as the appointment, what makes you think you can close something as major as the sale?

"Suppose after obtaining the appointment, you assess the needs of the prospect. Now it requires a follow-up call and the need to meet your builder. You still have not concluded a sales transaction, so the sale you make is the follow-up appointment. This in itself requires closing skills."

I further explained to Donna, "Salespeople are constantly closing and gaining commitments. Commitment and minor-point closings that occur during the sales process could be as simple as determining a need and ensuring their companies will satisfy that need. Selling, whether by one-call closing or through multiple-call contacts, is occurring during the entire presentation. *The presentation is actually the process of gaining commitment and closing.*"

The most appropriate times to close are during a presentation and at the end of it. You don't put off asking for the order later in the day or week. After the presentation, maybe during, the prospect usually has 100 percent of the information available and is more emotionally closer to making a decision than at any other time.

Have Your Closing Material With You...Always

Richard, an accomplished salesperson, excitedly proclaimed he had landed an oceanfront homesite sale that would net a $17,500 commission. I congratulated Richard, and asked for the contracts and deposit check so that we could process the paperwork. "Oh," he said, "I don't have them with me. As a matter of fact, I'm meeting the customer at the office in 30 minutes and we will prepare the contracts there."

I inquired, "Why didn't you prepare the agreements when you were with them?" I knew what his response would be.

"I didn't have contracts with me, but don't worry! They are solid. Besides, I would rather have the contracts typed."

I've experienced this scenario too many times but did not want to negate Richard's excitement.

In less than 10 minutes, Richard reappeared with the sullen look that required no explanation. The customer, now a prospect, had called with concerns over the investment property. They had decided to delay their decision and would not be coming to the office. Richard would meet them later in the day to give them the support information to pass on to their accountant.

Be ready to close anytime, anywhere—the moment your customer acknowledges acceptance. Keep your closing forms, calculator, pen and all other materials with you at all times. Take them with you wherever and whenever you are with a prospect.

Remember, you have worked hard moving a prospect past his fear of making a mistake (buyer's remorse in advance). If there is an interim period while you gather all your materials, doubts and fears have time to seep back into the prospect's mind, and the sale can unravel quickly.

When you receive commitment but decide to process the paperwork later, I promise you the client will have additional concerns you will have to address, and in some cases, you virtually will have to start your presentation over again. Do you really want to do that? As difficult as it is the first time around, the second time will be worse because the emotional odds will be against you.

Learn to Talk on Paper

I took this tip to heart from master salesperson and trainer Zig Ziglar. Zig suggests you always have a legal pad available during your presentation. He calls it "your talking pad."

Do you want to increase the power of your presentation twenty-two times, thus increase your probability of closing? Then learn to talk on paper. There's a reason there are twenty-two times more nerve endings from the eye to the brain versus the ear to the brain. Plus people naturally believe the written over the spoken word.

Ink it, don't think it. Delegate to document. When delivering a presentation, perform an interactive pad talk. In other words, display the presentation and its highlights in written form. The salesperson writes any key benefits, warranties and assurances on his or her talking pad and then lets the prospect view it during a planned oral presentation. Combine a verbal presentation with the power of the printed word.

When explaining finance and terms to your prospect, always use a calculator, not a pen or pencil. Buyers assume your numbers are indisputable when you actually do the math right in front of them.

To increase your closing effectiveness, always carry a legal binder, which contains your contracts, calculator, pen and any other materials necessary to close.

Ask and You Will Receive

Research conducted by Dr. Herb True of Notre Dame concludes that 46 percent of the people he interviewed ask for the order only once before giving up; 24 percent ask twice before shying away; 14 percent attempt to ask for the order the third time; and 12 percent continue to ask a fourth time before throwing in the towel. 96 percent of professional salespeople quit asking after one to four closing attempts.

What's startling is the same research indicates that 60 percent of all sales occur after the fifth attempt of asking for the order. It's conclusive. The top four percent of salespeople, who possess the courage and skills to ask for the order again after five previous attempts, are making 60 percent of the sales *as well as the commission.*

A Detroit newspaper reported a huge insurance policy had been purchased by Henry Ford. A friend of Mr. Ford's, who was also an insurance salesperson, was naturally upset and inquired why he did not buy from him.

Pay attention! Mr. Ford's answer holds the secret of sales success for anyone selling anything! Ford replied, "You didn't ask me."

Those of you who are hesitant to ask for fear of appearing like hard-sell, high-pressure salespeople, should know that asking for the order is the fundamental quality of the top new home and neighborhood sales professional. The critical closing instruction is to **ask for the order**. Ask enthusiastically. Ask confidently. And continue to ask until your invitation to own is accepted. Then have your paperwork ready.

Irene Buckley began selling insurance in the 1930s. In 1990, she was 95 and still selling. There was one January, she said, when she slowed down a little because she fell and broke a bone in her upper arm. She had to go to the doctor, and while she was there, sold him a $50,000 life insurance policy. Since she always had her paperwork with her, she signed him up on the spot.

THE FINAL INSTRUCTION...SILENCE

> *The only pressure you are allowed to use in a sales presentation is the pressure of silence after you have asked the closing question.*
> ~ **Brian Tracy**

When you ask a closing question, it's critical that you become perfectly silent and wait for the answer. Sounds easy, doesn't it? It was a difficult discipline for me to master and it's a challenge to convey its importance to most new salespeople.

Why is it necessary to remain silent after asking a closing question? If you say anything prior to receiving a response, you take the pressure off the prospect. By remaining silent, one of two things will occur:

- Your prospect answers the closing question, committing to own.

- Your prospect answers the closing question, giving you the reason(s) he will not own.

Either answer is acceptable. If he commits, it's just a matter of completing the paperwork. If he does not commit, you know why. This allows you the opportunity to overcome the objections (not conditions) and continue with the closing process until you conclude the sale.

WHAT ARE CLOSING TECHNIQUES?

To understand what closing is, let's discuss what closing is *not*.

Closing techniques **are not** tactics of the cunning used to manipulate people into purchasing homes they can't afford or don't want to own, in a neighborhood where that they don't want to live.

Closing is a skill the professional salesperson possesses that leads people to make decisions that benefit them. Understand, the closing technique is designed to move the decision-makers past a moment of tension, indecision or fear.

13

CLOSING TECHNIQUES: THE BAKER'S DOZEN

Even if you fall on your face, you're still moving forward.

~ Gallagher

❧   ❧   ❧

How many times do you ask for the order before the person says yes? As stated previously, statistics clearly indicate that closing usually occurs after the fifth attempt.

This is critical knowledge. If it takes a minimum of five closes to succeed, you won't lead a buyer to "yes" if you have only one or two closing techniques. When people ask me how many closing techniques they should memorize, I reply, "The Superachiever normally has a dozen-plus closing strategies committed to memory."

You may think, "Why so many?" I suggest a dozen-plus techniques because every buying situation is unique, and each buyer's personality is different.

Keep this in mind when deciding how many closing techniques you need to memorize.

If it takes more than five attempts to conclude a sale, that means multiple techniques must be learned. Look at it this way: If you receive more objections than you have responses, you will not get very far. Therefore, the reason you possess multiple techniques is to have more closes than they have objections. Use up their "no's" to lead them to "yes."

To get you started, here are 13 of the most powerful and proven closing techniques available to help your prospects agree to buy. I suggest you learn the following closes word for word.

UP THEIR "NO'S" WITH THE PROPER CLOSE

1. The Order Form Close

This is the fundamental closing technique. First, always have your contracts and forms with you at all times. If you work from your desk, display them. If you keep your paperwork in sight, the prospects know you are not trying to hide anything. And they become accustomed to seeing them if they come to your office more than once. It's also easier for you, if you have the necessary paperwork handy at the moment of closing. When you are delivering your presentation away from your desk, have a binder or attaché case containing your legal pad and contracts.

Why is the Order Form Close so effective? As you fill out the paperwork, you are not directly asking the prospect to buy (make a decision). Instead, you are making the decision for him.

The best times to work with this close are at the beginning and during your presentation. My favorite time to begin the Order Form Close is when the prospect asks a question that indicates a buying signal. You answer the question with a question of your own, and record the answer on the order form.

Prospect: "Is it possible to delay the closing date to 60 days?"

Superachiever: "Mr. Prospect, would an additional 30 days be more convenient?"

Prospect: "I'll need that time to secure additional funds."

Superachiever: "Let me make a note of that." Record the information on your order blank or contract.

As long as the prospect does not stop you from recording the answers on the contract, he is buying. However, the prospect may stop you by saying something like:

Prospect: "Is that a contract? (Or) You are ahead of yourself. I'm not buying anything."

Superachiever: "Of course you're not. I would never expect you to own without all the facts. I use this form to write all the information down. This form has everything about the offer arranged in a precise manner, such as price, terms, added features, and delivery date—all the information you and I both need for your review later. That's okay, isn't it?"

From the start of the presentation to the end, "make a note" of all his questions and record terms on the order form. By the end of the presentation the contract is virtually completed and will only require a signature. Here's how this entire close is intended to work:

Prospect: "How much is the down payment?"

Superachiever: "Mr. Prospect, we would require an initial investment of either 10 or 20 percent. Which would you prefer?"

Prospect: "I'd like to get in for the least amount. I suppose 10 percent."

Superachiever: "Great. Let me make a note of that."

Prospect: "Is that a contract? You're getting ahead of yourself. I'm not ready to buy."

Superachiever: "Of course you're not. I would never expect you to own without all the facts. This form has everything about the offering arranged in a precise manner, such as price, terms, added features, delivery date—all the information you and I both need for your review purposes later. That's okay, isn't it?"

Prospect: "Well, I guess that's okay."

Superachiever: "By the way, Mr. Prospect, we could schedule delivery of your new home in 120 days, if that fits into your time frame."

Prospect: "Actually, I need to be moved from my existing home in 90 days."

Superachiever: "Mr. Prospect, I'm going to make note that delivery must coordinate at the same time of your move."

Prospect: "Yes, that would work."

Superachiever: "Mr. Prospect, would this purchase be under your personal name or is anyone else appearing on the deed?"

Prospect: "It would be under both my wife's and my name."

Superachiever: "Outstanding! And your middle initial is?"

Prospect: "It's T."

Superachiever: "What is the correct spelling of your mailing address?"

When you have asked all the questions and the contract is completely filled out, you review the notes with the prospect and, if he agrees, ask him to authorize or okay the agreement.

∽   ∽   ∽

2. The I-Want-to-Think-About-It Close

Sales trainer Tom Hopkins has his students memorize this technique word for word in his three-day boot camp sessions, and I personally feel if you do not commit this particular close to memory you simply are not serious about the sales profession.

"I want to think about it" and "I want to think it over" are the most common objections a salesperson will encounter, regardless of the product offered. In the best of situations, under the most ideal conditions, you will hear these at least 50 percent of the time, so start committing this close to memory right away!

The prospects say "I want to think it over" for three reasons:

A. It's a Brush Off: Now swallow your ego and accept the fact that this prospect doesn't want what you're offering. Frequently the prospect will say "I want to think it over" because it's a nice way for him to send you on your way without hurting your feelings. The average salesperson is so vain he actually believes the prospect wakes up in the morning and goes to bed at night thinking over his offer. But, in reality, when the salesperson calls back two or three days later sure of a sale, the prospect doesn't even know who he is.

Now, suppose you are working with a genuinely interested prospect who tells you "I want to think about it." This is what is occurring with the interested prospect who is hesitating.

B. Buyer's Remorse in Advance: A new home is the decision of a lifetime and at the moment of closing the prospect experiences tension. The tension is a fear of making a mistake, buying the wrong floor plan, paying too much or even being criticized by friends. These fears cause him to back away at the moment of closing and say, "I want to think about it."

C. Financial Resources: He tells you he wants to think about it because of the price or terms surrounding the home or homesite. Don't be fooled. Usually the only reason he tells you "I want to think about it" is because he wonders if he can or should be able to afford your home or homesite.

The problem with "I want to think about it" is that it's a broad statement, not narrowed to any one specific concern. You are not down to the final objection and have nothing concrete to overcome. If you will follow this procedure, you will move beyond the vague generality of "thinking about it" to the final objection.

Prospect: "I need to think it over."

Superachiever: "That's fine. Obviously you would not take the time to think about it unless you were genuinely interested, would you?" (Remain silent and wait for his reply. This question confirms he is genuinely interested.)

Prospect: "Oh, yeah, I'm definitely interested."

Superachiever: "Great, since you are interested, I can assume you will give this careful consideration, won't you?" (Remain silent and wait for the reply. His response, if he says yes, confirms he will actually think about it.)

Prospect: "Yes, I definitely will be giving it the consideration it deserves."

Superachiever: "Outstanding! Just to clarify my thinking, what phase of the offer is it you will be considering? Is it the area?"

Prospect: "No, the community, location is perfect."

Superachiever: "Could it be the neighborhood?"

Prospect: "No. We love the neighborhood."

Superachiever: "Mr. Prospect, I sense you hesitating. Do you mind my asking if it's something to do with the money?"

Be assured if he has come this far and he is still genuinely interested, in most instances, it will be a money issue that is hindering progress. This being the case, bridge to the Money Close on page 166. Internalize and memorize it.

Here is the "I-Want-to-Think-About-It Close":

Superachiever: "That's fine. Obviously you wouldn't take the time to think about it unless you were genuinely interested, would you? Since you are genuinely interested, I can assume you will give this careful consideration. Just to clarify my thinking, what phase of the offer will you be considering? Is it the area? Is it the neighborhood? I sense your hesitancy. Do you mind my asking, is it the money?"

Here is the key. Prospects do not think about your offer after they leave. They do not review your literature and product information. What they do is move on with their lives. The time to nail down the sale is at the end of your presentation after you have identified their needs and clearly presented your neighborhood as the solution to those needs.

❧   ❧   ❧

3. Assumptive Close

All top sales professionals are assumptive closers. From the beginning of the presentation to the end, they confidently *assume* the buyer will own even before they have received confirmation or acknowledgment that a buying decision has been reached.

The Assumptive Close is sometimes referred to as "The next-step close." Have you ever been in the middle of your presentation and the prospect says, "What's the next step?" It may not happen often but when it does, it's time to be assumptive. Swing into the Order Form Close and begin wrapping up the details.

Prospect: "What's the next step?"

Superachiever: "Mr. & Mrs. Prospect, I'm glad you asked. The next step is for you to authorize the agreements, and I will need a check for $5,000 as the deposit on your new homesite."

If the prospect does not ask what the next step is, then initiate the Assumptive Close at the end of your sales presentation by first issuing a Trial Close.

Superachiever: "Mr. & Mrs. Prospect, do you have any additional questions before we begin the paperwork?"

Prospects: "No."

Superachiever: "Great. Then the next step is for you to authorize the agreements as well as prepare a check for $5,000 as a deposit on your brand new home."

Pay strict attention! You have just been given the most powerful Assumptive Close in your sales career. That is the strategy of the "No Close." This close was developed by Master Sales Educator Bob Schultz and actually elicits the response a salesperson fears most, which is "No." With this technique, you gently nudge the prospect into saying no.

Superachiever: "Do you have any questions before we begin the paperwork?"

Prospect: "No."

Superachiever: "Great. Then the next step is for you to authorize the agreements and make out a check for $5,000 as a deposit on your investment."

From here you simply begin processing the contracts. You would be surprised at the vast numbers of prospects who agree to "yes" by saying "no." If, for any reason the prospect does object, you overcome the objection and then ask for the order again.

To be an assumptive closer, the sale must first occur in your mind before it occurs in the prospect's mind. Its power is in the psychological principle that your assumptive attitude creates the prospect's desire for your product. The stronger your positive assumptive attitude that the sale is inevitable, the greater the probability the prospect will own.

ASSUMPTIVE CLOSES TO MEMORIZE

Superachiever: "Mr. Prospect, prior to our meeting I took the liberty of preparing the paperwork. All that is needed is for you to authorize the agreements."

Superachiever: "We seem to be in agreement on all the major points. The initial investment is only $5,000. Would you be taking care of that with a personal check?"

The Assumptive Handshake Close
(A Variation on the Assumptive Close)

Since the beginning of time, the handshake represents a person's word and integrity, and psychologically bonds an agreement.

Larry, a super salesperson, concluded an expensive vacation home transaction with an assumptive handshake. At the end of the presentation, after making countless objections, the husband looked to his wife and said, "What do you think?" The chances were high the wife would respond with, "I think we should think it over." Before a reply was given, however, Larry looked at them both and offered his assurances. "I think you have made a wise decision. Congratulations." He then shook hands with both the husband and the wife and they accepted.

It's important to note the buyers were qualified, their needs determined, and the solution was presented. Here, as in most cases,

158

there was hesitancy. The moment of tension was relieved and the sale concluded by the Assumptive Handshake Close.

∽ ∽ ∽

4. Alternatives Close

This close automatically concludes the sale by offering the prospect two or more alternatives. You offer a choice between something and something rather than a choice between something and nothing.

Earlier we discussed, in depth, the buyer's fears and that "no" is usually a natural ingrained response—a knee-jerk reaction. You never ask the prospect, "Do you want this or not?" This allows the prospect to say "no." Instead, you say, "Would you prefer item A or B?" Either answer (item A or item B) is a "yes" decision.

Depending upon the circumstances, there are several ways to present an Alternatives Close.

■ **Delivery:**

Closing on your new homesite will occur in 30 or 60 days. Which would you prefer?

■ **Finances:**

The initial investment can be secured by cash or personal check. Which would you prefer?

■ **Included or added features:**

Which do you feel would best compliment your new kitchen, the oak or maple cabinets?

■ **Appointments:**

I have either Monday or Wednesday available for this week. What works better for you? How about 10 a.m. or 12 noon for lunch?

Learn to offer two choices to your prospect. Ask, "Do you want this or do you want that?" When the question is answered, it's the perfect opportunity to "make a note" which leads you to your Order Form Close.

∽ಎ   ∽ಎ   ∽ಎ

5. Trial Close

The purpose of the Trial Close is to evaluate and determine where you are with your prospect during the presentation. It's a way to check the water before you dive in.

Unlike a close that concludes the transaction, a Trial Close is not asking for the order and the money, but merely seeking the prospect's opinion and the willingness to own. Actually, asking for opinions (Trial Close) is something you perform throughout the presentation. Here are examples:

- ❑ How are we doing so far?

- ❑ Is this what you had in mind?

- ❑ Is this what you are looking for?

- ❑ Does this make sense to you?

The benefit of the Trial Close is that the prospect can answer yes or no. Because you are merely "testing the waters," you don't end the presentation. Great salespeople use this technique throughout the presentation to take the prospect's "buying temperature."

"Mr. and Mrs. Prospect, is this what you are looking for?" If they say no, you say, "Fine, what is it you are looking for?" They confirm and you move to the next fork in the road. "You like the oak or pine trim?"

Then you move to the next fork, "Is this what you like?" Then follow the road to the final close.

The basic process of selling is asking questions, determining hot buttons, and gaining commitments. Trial Closes solidify the questions you ask.

TRIAL CLOSES TO MEMORIZE:

Superachiever: "I get the impression you are excited about the privacy of the homesite. Is that correct?"

Superachiever: "Mr. & Mrs. Prospect, on a scale of 1 to 10—1 meaning owning in our neighborhood may not make complete sense yet, and 10 being it makes perfect sense—where are you on the scale?"

Prospect: "I guess we're at a seven."

Superachiever: "Great. What additional information will you need to help you get to a 10?"

Superachiever: "Now that I have demonstrated the features and benefits of our new homes, how do they compare with what you've seen elsewhere?"

Superachiever: "Mr. Prospect, why is it you want to own in the community?"

Superachiever: "After playing our golf course and having your family experience the lifestyle of the neighborhood, wouldn't you agree it's unnecessary to even consider owning anywhere else?"

❧   ❧   ❧

6. Ben Franklin Close

Okay, I know what you are thinking. The Ben Franklin Close is as old as the hills. Everybody is familiar with it. However, this does not negate the fact that it's still the most powerful close that has ever been developed for the sales profession. And for good reason.

The Ben Franklin Close parallels how humans process information and think. Whenever we are faced with a decision, we run through a checks-and-balance system to weigh the pros and cons of the decision. We look for a reason to do something or not to do it.

Ben Franklin, who was America's first self-made millionaire, made decisions by first taking a piece of paper and drawing a line down the center. On one side he wrote all the reasons favoring the decision, and on the other side he wrote his reasons for opposing it. Then, he would review his list and render a careful decision.

The reason why salespeople fight this technique is because they think it's an outdated method. However, let's look at the *improved* Ben Franklin Close.

Superachiever: "Mr. & Mrs. Prospect, I can sense you are having difficulty with this decision, aren't you? (Silence, wait for reply.) The last thing I want is for you to make a choice you might be uncomfortable with. May I make a suggestion? Let's use a systematic decision-making method. On one side of my legal pad we will list the reasons favoring a positive decision, and on the other side, we'll list your concerns. Afterward, we'll see if it makes sense to you."

As the Superachiever, take your pen and paper and fill out all the reasons for owning. Then make a Summary Close (page 163) restating all the positive reasons for owning. You should be able to come up with countless reasons why they should buy in your community. After you fill out the positive reasons, you say, "It certainly seems as if there are a number of good reasons for going forward, doesn't it?" (Wait for the reply.)

Now you simply hand them the pen and paper and say, "Now that we've listed all the reasons for proceeding, can you think of any reasons not to go ahead?" The key now is to remain perfectly silent and let them work on it by themselves. Most of the time, they will not be able to list more than three or four reasons to prohibit owning.

From here you begin to Assumptively Close by saying, "It looks like you have made the right decision," or "It seems pretty obvious, doesn't it?" Then progress to the Order Form Close.

The Ben Franklin Close should not be limited to the end of your presentation when you are trying to gain the final commitment. In my real estate development career, the home-building division was highly competitive, so when prospects suggested they were considering the services of another builder, I asked two questions that triggered a Ben Franklin Close.

Superachiever: "Mr. & Mrs. Prospect, builder XYZ does a fine job. I'm curious. Can you tell me what services and features he offers that make you to want to do business with him? Are there any reasons or concerns that would cause you not to have that company construct your dream home?" The first purpose for asking the questions is to understand their hot buttons (everything they are looking for in a builder). The second purpose is to learn about what is called the "inverse hot button"— the reasons why they would not want to use a particular builder. From this, you can develop your presentation to utilize their hot buttons, as well as address their concerns.

This is a magnificent close. When a person has difficulty making a decision, normally he has moved past his emotional high and is attempting to justify the purchase through logic. The improved Ben Franklin Close will satisfy even the most discriminating, analytical person.

❦   ❦   ❦

7. The Summary Close

When you approach the end of your presentation, the prospect is faced with arranging all of your information into a clear and concise picture prior to rendering a decision.

As I stated before, you are always selling benefits, and you must summarize them in a manner that proves your product meets your prospect's needs. This will raise her buying temperature just before you ask for the order.

Here is a four-step process to develop your Summary Close.

Step 1—Bridge into your Summary Close with a transition statement.

Ms. Prospect, we have covered a lot of territory today! Before moving forward, let's review the highlights of our discussion.

Step 2—Reconfirm your prospect's wants, needs and desires.

You mentioned (community name's) location was ideally situated, close to your work. Is that correct?

Your primary concern was the school district and you seem satisfied with the information I've provided in regards to their testing scores and ratings. Is that on target?

And, of course, the amenities and security our neighborhood offers suit your lifestyle. Have I included everything?

Step 3—Summarize how your product or service meets the prospect's wants, needs and desires.

For your convenience, we will schedule an appointment today with a local financial institution and they can begin processing your loan application. From here, I would like to suggest that you meet with our design department and they can assist you in coordinating the custom features you want to include in your new home.

Step 4—Ask for the order and close the sale (Tie-down)

The only remaining small detail is preparation of the paperwork and I've taken the liberty to prepare the agreements in advance. All that's necessary is your authorization.

A common question aspiring Superachievers ask is how to actually transition to the final closing sequence. The Summary Close is the perfect method to "bridge" into your final close. You summarize the benefits, even if there are as many as 20 or more items, and say, "When would you like to get started?" or "The initial investment is 10 percent. Will that be cash or check?" If acceptance is gained, you simply conclude the sale with the Order Form Close. If an objection is offered, you identify and overcome the final objection, thus closing the sale.

🔊   🔊   🔊

8. The Reduction-to-the-Ridiculous Close (Cost-Per-Day Close)

There is a world of difference between willingness to pay and ability to pay. Therefore, when you use the "Calculate the Cost-Per-Day Close," it bridges the gap between willingness and ability to pay.

Whether the objections are "It costs too much," or "It's more than I want to pay," or "I only have this much money budgeted," this closing method will easily overcome the money objection if you determine the difference in your price and spread the cost over a period of time.

For example, your homesite costs $95,000 and the prospect is offering to pay $87,000. The discrepancy between the two prices is only $8,000. They have committed to $87,000. The concern is $8,000 —the amount you have to justify. You simply spread the difference in price over the lifetime of ownership.

Superachiever: "Mr. Prospect, I appreciate your concern. $8,000 seems like a major amount until you break it down. (Hand the prospect your calculator and allow him to work through the math with you.) Let's say, hypothetically, you'll build your new home and live in it for 10 years. Does that sound reasonable?"

Prospect: "I suppose I would own it for 10 years."

Superachiever: "If we divide $8,000 by the ten years we get $800 per year, don't we? Now, let's divide $800 by 52 weeks per year, and we arrive at $15.38 per week. Isn't that correct? Of course, there are seven days per week so would you mind dividing $15.38 by 7? That's only $2.20 per day."

(Sometimes your prospect will say this is ridiculous, so before the objection surfaces, steal the objection in advance.)

Superachiever: "Mr. Prospect, I know this might seem ridiculous, but if you think about it, that $8,000 really isn't that much when you consider you could own what you really want and deserve for only $2.20 a day. You're not going to let $2.20 per day stand in the way, are you?"

A real pro used this technique on a friend who was purchasing a fine quality wristwatch. He truly wanted to buy a watch that was $2,050 more than he had budgeted.

This phenomenal salesperson, calculator in hand, said, "Mitch, a premier watch is an heirloom you will pass on to your son. But, for discussion's sake, let's say you only enjoy the watch ten years. That's only $205 per year or $3.94 per week. If we really break it down, it would only be 56 cents per day to own the watch you want rather than having to settle for something else."

❧   ❧   ❧

9. Oblique Comparison Close

From this point, the salesperson bridged to the Oblique Comparison Close: to compare the difference in price with something that seems inconsequential or minuscule. In this case, she used a soft drink as the oblique comparison.

"Mitch, I bet you probably spend more than 56 cents a day on soft drinks and coffee, don't you? For less than 56 cents, you could own what you deserve. By the way, will that be a personal check or charge?"

❧   ❧   ❧

10. The Money Close

For real estate, in which financial terms are offered, here is the procedure you can use every time to break the terms into component parts:

1. Total Investment	$_____
2. Initial Investment	$_____
3. Monthly Investment	$_____

Whenever a prospect says, "I need to think it over," in most cases the main concern is the money. Review the "I-Want-to-Think-About-It Close," on page 154.

Superachiever: "Mr. Prospect, I sense your hesitancy. Do you mind my asking if it is the money?"

Prospect: "Well, actually, it is a little more than we anticipated."

166

NOTE: *By breaking the money into component parts, you will determine if it is the total investment, monthly investment, or initial investment that is blocking the sale.*

Superachiever: "I can certainly understand, so why don't we take a look at the total offering."

    1. Total Investment: $_____

"You feel comfortable with the value of our homes? Am I correct?"

    2. Initial Investment: $_____

"Is that amount comfortable, or is that amount readily available?"

    3. Monthly Investment: $_____

"How does that work with your budget?"

Suppose, after running through this scenario, he is comfortable with the total investment and initial investment, but the monthly investment is the challenge. You may then be in a position to offer different terms or creative financing. "I can understand, Mr. Prospect. But just suppose I could offer extended terms—from 15 years to 20 years—and reduce the monthly investment by _____. Does that place it within your budget?"

What if he says it's the initial investment? (By the way, my father always told me that if it were not for the down payment, a salesperson could sell anything, because society is only concerned with, "How much per month?") You can say, "I understand, Mr. Prospect, the initial investment is a little more than you anticipated. So tell me how far apart we are. I'm working for you."

Of course, if he is comfortable with both the monthly investment and the initial investment, the total investment objection (price) can be overcome by showing value or using the Cost-Per-Day Close.

However, you must remember, when prospects hesitate over the price, and there are terms offered, it might not be the cost that places it out of reach. Your stumbling block could be in one of the components of the cost; specifically, total investment, monthly investment or initial investment.

Additional Price Responses

Your price is too high.

How did you arrive at that figure?

What did you think the value would be?

How high is too high?

You have to do better than that.

What do you mean better?

How far apart are we?

Are you saying you are <u>prepared</u> to own this home or homesite?

I can get a home for less from your competitor.

I can appreciate that, Mr. Prospect.

That being the case, why haven't you purchased from them yet?

> NOTE: *That's a bold response, but he will tell you what's keeping him from buying from the competition.*

11. The Sharp Angle Close

The Sharp Angle Close—sometimes referred to as the "If I could ... would you?" close—is a superb maneuver when confronted with most types of objections. Whatever the concern you receive, you simply "Sharp angle" the objection and send it back to the prospect with "If I could ...would you?"

Prospect: "I don't know if I can afford it."

Superachiever: "Mr. Prospect, if I could arrange convenient financial terms to make this possible, would you proceed forward?"

The Sharp Angle Close is also a perfect method to handle smoke-screen objections. I discussed in the objections portion of the book that sometimes the prospect's first objection may not be the real or final objection. Observe how to smoke out the hidden objection with "If I could ...would you?"

Prospect: "I don't know if I can afford it."

Superachiever: "Mr. Prospect, if I could arrange convenient financial terms to make this possible, would you proceed forward?"

Prospect: "Is that possible?"

(The average salesperson would be tempted to jump in and answer yes. The Superachiever takes the opportunity to make sure she's handled the final objection and is not so quick to answer.)

Superachiever: "I can't be certain until we process a loan application. I have an application, which will only take a moment to complete, and we can make the sale 'subject to' financial approval. That makes sense, doesn't it?"

Prospect: "I don't know. I probably need to think about it."

Superachiever: "Mr. Prospect, I sense your hesitancy. In addition to the financial arrangements, is there something else that prohibits you from becoming a new homeowner?"

Prospect: "Well, I just want to be certain I can include the additional features and landscaping as I've specified."

(The Superachiever now issues a second Sharp Angle Close)

Superachiever: "Mr. Prospect, I understand how you feel. In addition to the terms, if I could offer full written warranty assurances, would you proceed today?"

Prospect: "Well, under those terms, it seems reasonable."

NOTE: *The Superachiever now begins to conclude the sale by employing three additional closing techniques: the*

Assumptive Handshake Close, the Order Form Close, and the Alternatives Close.

Superachiever: "Congratulations Mr. Prospect! You've made a wise decision." (Assumptive Handshake Close)

Prospect: "Thank you."

Superachiever: The next step is to simply prepare the paperwork. "May I have the correct spelling of your full name?" (Order Form Close)

Prospect: "John A. Smith."

Superachiever: "Mr. Smith, about the initial investment, will you be handling the deposit with cash or personal check?" (Alternatives Close)

Prospect: "Personal check."

Closes Are Stacked on Top of One Another

It is vitally important that you review the previous closing scenario numerous times because it has an important underlying lesson. Realize that, although we began with the Sharp Angle Close, this was not the technique that concluded the sale. The Sharp Angle Close was only a preceding close that led to the final closing strategies of the Assumptive Handshake Close, Order Form Close and Alternatives Close.

Take heed and pay close attention to the next statement. The importance of knowing multiple closing techniques is because *no one close concludes the sale.* It requires the use of many closing techniques.

You will notice we layered technique upon technique, each close building upon the preceding close, until the sale was complete. We never directly asked the prospect to buy. We led him to the decision with closing questions. Let's review.

■ *I can't afford it.*

170

Sharp Angle–If I could arrange the terms, would you proceed today?

■ *How can I be certain of the added features and landscaping?*

Sharp Angle–If I could offer written assurances, would you go forward today?

■ *I need to think about it.*

Think-About-It Close—In addition to that, is there anything else?

Assumptive Handshake Close—Congratulations and assurances

Order Form Close—Assumptively closing

Alternatives Close—Asking for the money — cash or check

As you can see, many techniques were employed:

1. & 2. Sharp Angle Close

3. Think-About-It Close

4. Assumptive Handshake Close

5. Order Form Close

6. Alternatives Close

Remember the statistics that revealed the average sale is concluded after the fifth attempt? Asking for the order and getting it requires employing specific techniques and having a preplanned, scripted methodology to guide the buyer into a beneficial decision that normally would have been prohibited by his or her own fears.

◈   ◈   ◈

12. The Yes Momentum Close

This great close consists of asking your prospects questions that lead them to answer yes. Superachievers know that, if their prospects get into a mental pattern of saying yes from the very beginning of their presentation, it will become very difficult for them to say no at the moment of closing.

The goal of the Yes Momentum Close is to create an atmosphere of agreement. To do this, you first need to tie down the close by asking questions that, at the beginning or at the end of the sentence, demand a yes answer. It psychologically ties your prospect into a "yes" agreement.

Whenever you state anything about your neighborhood, company or service, the prospect has a tendency to disbelieve you. It's your job to present your offer in the best light. Tom Hopkins says, "If you say it, they doubt it. If they say it, it's true." Therefore, the benefit of a tie-down is that the prospect verbally agrees with your statements, and then comes to believe what she is saying.

Tie-Down Words

Doesn't it	Hasn't she
Isn't that right	Won't they
Wasn't it	Aren't they
Couldn't it	Shouldn't it
Wouldn't it	Can't you
Aren't you	Don't you agree
Won't you	Isn't it
Haven't they	Didn't it

Types of Tie-Downs

■ **Deductive Tie-Downs** are the most common and are used at the end of a sentence to demand yes.

Superachiever: "This homesite is a tremendous value, wouldn't you agree?"

Prospect: "Yes."

■ **Inverted Tie-Downs** occur at the beginning of a sentence. It is less demanding and leads a prospect to say yes.

Superachiever: "Isn't it exactly what you have in mind?"

Prospect: "Yes."

- **Internal Tie-Downs** are used in the middle of your statements of fact.

Superachiever: "Mr. and Mrs. Prospect, as we stand here on the deck, can't you imagine how you and your family will enjoy this new home for years to come?"

Prospects: "Yes."

- **Tag-On Tie-Downs:** Whenever your prospect offers positive statements, add a tie-down in your response that bolsters value.

Prospect: "The views are absolutely incredible!"

Superachiever: "Aren't they?"

Start your presentation and conversation positively, and lead your prospect to agreement beginning with your greeting. "Welcome. Thank you for the opportunity to meet. It's a great day, isn't it?" Eliciting numerous, small agreements from the beginning of your presentation to the end will lead you to the final positive close: "This is what you want, isn't it?"

Examples of Tie-Downs

I bet you are surprised with how affordable new home ownership is, aren't you?

Isn't this the kind of home you have always dreamed of owning?

It's a sound investment, wouldn't you agree?

Based on what we have shared, our community satisfies your lifestyle perfectly, doesn't it?

13. My Banker, Accountant, Lawyer or Third-Party Close

We have all had a prospect tell us our offer seemed to be the perfect solution, but before making a final decision, he says, "I need to run this by my banker (Realtor, parents or child)."

When a prospect says he needs a third-party approval, either he is using a smoke-screen objection or he is controlled by his fears.

If obtaining advice from a third party, such as a financial advisor, is a valid objection, then recognize the prospect's fears. When the prospect says, "I cannot make a decision without seeking the approval of an outside advisor," he simply needs someone to assure him it's a wise decision.

The Third-Party Close incorporates the closing strategy of "subject to" or "conditional-terms" selling.

Prospect: "This seems to be the perfect home/homesite but, before making my final decision, I need to run this by my banker (or accountant)."

Superachiever: "I can understand. Then am I correct in assuming you are totally satisfied, and there is no question in your mind that you feel it's the right thing for you to do?"

Prospect: "Yes, I'm satisfied. I just want her to look it over."

Superachiever: "Great, then the only question is whether your banker or accountant says it's the right thing to do. Is that correct?"

Prospect: "That's it."

Superachiever: "Mr. Prospect, may I ask you a question? (pause) Just suppose your banker/accountant were present at this very moment, and she advised you to take advantage of the offering. Would you act today?"

Prospect: "I suppose I would."

Superachiever: "Unfortunately, she is not with us today. But prior to your speaking with her and in order to facilitate the transaction in a timely fashion, let's prepare the paperwork now and we will make the sale "subject to" her final approval. This way the process has begun and if by chance she doesn't agree, we will simply start over. That makes perfect sense, doesn't it?"

If the prospect agrees to the paperwork "subject to," you are now involved in the process and you can facilitate the details of the sale with the lawyer, accountant or advisor, answering questions and overcoming the third-party's objections personally.

A CLOSING THOUGHT

Every profession in the world has its own rate of failure. Yet, sales is the only profession in the world where the standard, normal rate of failure can be 80 to 90 percent. In the best of times, four out of five calls will end in NO. And in tough economic times, when the competition is vicious, the rate is even greater.

In my estimation, the difference between failure and success is perception. Your perception will always be your reality. Therefore, do not perceive "failure" as anything other than a necessary learning experience that must occur for you to achieve success. The Superachiever perceives failure as an opportunity to grow and continue to move forward. Malcolm Forbes said, "Even failure is success if we learn from it."

If you become discouraged, remember:

- ☐ Cy Young, baseball's most revered pitcher, only won 511 games out of the 906 he pitched.

- ☐ Babe Ruth, before achieving the home-run record, first held the record for strikeouts.

- ☐ Michael Jordan, the celebrated basketball superstar, was cut from his high school team for one year.

- ☐ Thomas Edison failed 10,000 times before he succeeded in creating the incandescent light.

❑   Colonel Sanders (of Kentucky Fried Chicken) was retired and more than 60 years old before he decided to make his recipe known. He made close to 1,000 calls and spent nights in his car before he made his first sale.

❑   Walt Disney was fired from a job because his boss said he never had any creative ideas.

It is critical to understand that, as you attempt to master the many closing techniques, you risk failure. This is true while attempting anything new. I will assure you it's all right to fail when first trying the closing techniques, but it's not all right to avoid learning and mastering the techniques. Failure is not your enemy. Complacency and lack of initiative are your enemies. You might think you cannot fail if you do not try. But if you do not try, then by default, you have already failed.

Realize your success will come as you improve through practice, learning, memorizing, internalizing and selling to a process.

Take these proven principles, techniques, methods and strategies and persist. And if you will persist, I promise you will achieve the success you want and so richly deserve.

"Don't Quit"

Life is queer with its twists and turns,

As everyone of us sometimes learns;

And many a failure turns about,

When he might have won had he stuck it out.

Don't give up though the race seems slow;

You may succeed with another blow.

Success is failure turned inside out,
The silver tint of the clouds of doubt;
And you can never tell how close you are;
It may be near when it seems so far.
So stick to the fight when you're hardest hit.
It's when things seem worse,
That you must not quit.

— Author unknown —

14

STEP 8 OF THE POWER PROCESS: DO YOU GIVE UP OR CLEAN UP ON FOLLOW UP?

It is always too early to quit.

~ Norman Vincent Peale

Once you have sold a customer, make sure he is satisfied with your goods. Stay with him until the goods are used up or worn out. Your product may be of such long life that you will never sell him again, but he will sell you and your product to his friends.

~ Businessman William Feather

I don't measure a man's success by how high he climbs, but by how high he bounces when he hits bottom.

~ General George Patton

          ⚘   *⚘*   *⚘*

The undeniable truth is most new home or homesite sales occur as a result of multiple contacts.

Follow up is not an effort to negate the fact that many prospects will choose to own on their first visit. And certainly follow up is not an exercise to diminish the results of those salespeople and communities that achieve a high ratio of first-time buying decisions. It's just important to understand that the nature of our business requires multiple calls, and most sales are completed on return visits to the community, usually after the prospect has already shopped and, by the process of exclusion, crossed all other competitive offerings off her list.

179

FOLLOW UP: Covert Your Contacts Into Contracts

Since research indicates the average sale requires five contacts before converting the prospect into a customer, the Superachiever who possesses the courage and technical ability to follow up and follow through to the fifth contact will make the lion's share of the sales as well as the commissions.

So, if this is what it takes to make a sale, are you currently contacting and calling on your prospects an average of five times after they visit your sales center? And do you presently have a system, backed with a proven process, to maintain the contact until the prospect is converted into a customer?

Before continuing, let's define follow up. According to Webster, follow up means (a) to pursue closely and tenaciously; (b) to increase the effectiveness by further action or repetition; (c) to pursue to a solution or conclusion.

When you tenaciously pursue what your customers need until solutions are found, your effectiveness as a salesperson increases. That is what follow up is all about. *It is exceeding your customer's expectations in advance.* Your service is so good prior to their owning, there is no question your prospect will do business with you and your company.

A good example of anticipating the customer's needs and following up to meet those needs is found by studying how the Ritz-Carlton Hotel Company operates. If any customer has a complaint about any part of the hotel's operation, each employee is authorized by management to use his or her best judgment to satisfy the customer. To do this, the employee may spend up to $2,000 of the *company's money* per incident.

In practical application, this means that a guest who isn't satisfied with a meal may, at the discretion of the waiter, have the price removed from the bill. The front desk clerk may place a guest in an upgraded room at the least expensive price. And for the hotel guest in town for a week on business, the concierge may provide tickets to see a favorite show gratis.

This freedom to satisfy is expressed in other ways. A customer suffering from a cold is sent a complimentary pitcher of orange juice. A bellman surprises a guest by having her car washed and detailed, at no charge, because she has an important meeting to attend and doesn't have the time to have it done herself.

Taking service one step further—and this is where anticipating customer needs is evident—the hotel chain installed an extensive computer database that tracks every repeat customer's likes and dislikes. A businessman who does not care for alcoholic beverages finds his room's wet bar stocked with soft drinks, juices and his preferred brand of bottled water. If another guest wants a country ham and soft boiled egg breakfast served at 7 a.m. each morning, along with the local newspaper, he has it, regardless of whether he is at a Ritz in California or Australia.

Called the Repeat Guest Program, this system identifies a guest's preferences and accommodates them. Considering there are approximately 500,000 repeat customers, this is not an easy task. But the hotel's president believes it's worth the $700,000 a year it takes to run the computer system because he understands that building a business depends upon building relationships.

The success of The Ritz-Carlton illustrates two points. First, follow up works and, second, so does a system.

Following is a system containing 12 proactive follow-up strategies that will *exceed your customer's expectations in advance*. Before diving into the strategies, we need to identify the six methods or tools you have at your immediate disposal to use in following up and converting your contacts into contracts. Unfortunately, most salespeople only utilize one or two of these methods and never incorporate the six together. In this chapter, you will discover how to integrate the six methods and 12 strategies simultaneously. Each one of these will make your customers have a sense of your presence in their lives.

METHODS OR TOOLS USED TO FOLLOW UP A SALE

- **Product literature:** Your company probably has a variety of product information—such as brochures, handouts, video presentations and technical data—to assist with your follow up. Product literature released in a controlled fashion is the ideal method for securing appointments.

- **Mail:** You follow up a sale by mailing letters, cards, notes as well as your product literature. Your mission is to convert ordinary mail into a personal contact.

- **Telephone:** A powerful tool as long as you know how to use it. Gaining a complete understanding of how to properly use the phone to your best advantage will create additional sales that might otherwise be lost to your competition.

- **Facsimile:** The fax is a wonderful method of follow up. Why? Because people may creatively use their voice mail and electronic answering services to avoid your calls, and often will avoid reading your mail. But the fax has a sense of urgency, and most people will respond to, or at least read, a fax.

- **E-Mail:** Rapid advances in wired and wireless technologies, new software and the broad use of desktop and laptop computers have spurred electronic mail to the forefront of communication.

- **Appointments:** Appointments are the goal of follow up. Every method you engage—whether it's the phone, fax, e-mail, letters and/or product literature—is designed to place you in front of a qualified buyer.

Now that we have established the six methods or tools of follow up, we need to establish a way of using the system. If you take the six methods and combine them with the 12 strategies, you will have the ingredients necessary to proactively follow up with a customer all the way through your sale's cycle.

STRATEGY #1: Follow Up is the Process of Building a Business Relationship.

Someone once told me, "In business, reputations are longer in the making than in the losing."

Your success in new home and neighborhood sales is determined by your ability to not only form a valued business relationship with a customer, but to maintain it.

The marketplace is uncertain. The customer is inundated with choices. Every salesperson who makes contact with your prospect has dollar signs in his or her eyes. What your customer needs, and wants, is stability. You can provide that.

Establishing a strong business relationship is essential. The customer seeks someone he or she can trust before deciding which home or homesite to purchase. Your customers want the assurance that they can rely on you to fulfill the commitments of the builder/developer after the money has changed hands.

In a neighborhood sale, the relationship between you and your customers is continuous. Before they purchase in your community, they are largely independent. But the moment they sign on the bottom line and own in your neighborhood, they become dependent on the warranties and assurances you have given them.

Because purchasing a new home or homesite is long-lasting, the relationship will be long-term. Initially the relationship is far more significant than the home or homesite. Since customers view products and services as commodities available from any source, they always have the ability to choose between competing builders and developers. Therefore, before they decide *where* to buy, they are going to decide *from whom* to buy. The salesperson they most trust will be the one they select.

Because the business relationship is so vitally important, you should tell your customers that your personal goal and the company's mission is to enter into a long-term, mutually-beneficial business relationship. Offer subtle reassurances that you will be there for them long after the ink dries. Then make every effort to keep your word.

STRATEGY #2: The Responsibility of the Appointment is Yours.

Have you ever said to a potential customer these seven deadly words: "Come back any time. I'm always here."? Do you realize how you have destroyed your chance for a sale? Tell somebody to "come back anytime" and you deplete every ounce of urgency you may have created. But more importantly, you have just informed the prospect that you are a nonprofessional who sits around all day with nothing better to do than wishing and hoping for business to come your way. That reminds me of a poem I heard:

Sitting here and wishing, makes no person great. The good Lord sends the fish, but you must dig the bait.

In the appointment phase of the follow-up process, you must understand that you can't close the sale without a "next appointment." Proactively speaking, this means unless the prospect purchases at that moment, the sales call must continue and you and your prospect must be committed to one another.

Your commitment to follow up is the promise to provide further information to keep the sales process moving forward. Yet, commitment is a two-way street. Therefore, your prospect must have an understanding of what he or she also must do to move the process along. Commitment from a prospect means specifically making an appointment, which is subliminally saying, "I will set aside this time for you to teach me more about (what could be) my new home." A vague promise to "think about it" or to "get back with you next week" is no commitment at all.

What you want at the end of the sales call is a promise to take some action by a specific date. The prospect's promise to action demonstrates to you they are willing to invest their time and resources, just as you are. The fundamental issue is time. When you agree to commit your time and resources (through follow up) without getting something in return (appointment), you are saying, "My time is not as valuable as yours."

The first step is for you to take personal responsibility for the appointment and, from this point forward, never leave the appointment to chance. What do I mean by leaving the appointment to chance? Have you ever had a prospect say, by phone or in person, "I'll call you back" or "I'll be in touch"? With this in mind, let me share with you a new weight-loss program to try. It's guaranteed to work. The next time your customer comments, "I'll call you back," resolve to miss every meal until they do. Follow this plan, and either you will be thinner or you will thin out your customer base by working only with those willing to make a commitment.

It isn't the responsibility of the prospects to come or call back. They normally won't do it. They will either forget, procrastinate, get sidetracked or, even worse, get involved with another salesperson. They must have the discipline of another appointment. That's why it's important for you to initiate all callbacks, contacts and appointments.

Here's how to do it. The next time your prospect suggests he will call you back, take control of the situation and say, "Mr. Prospect, it would be easier if I contacted you. I'm busy, in and out of the office, virtually impossible to reach, so I'll call you back. When is a convenient time to speak again?"

If they suggest they will be coming back at a later date without a specific appointment say, "Mr. Prospect, we are extremely busy with interested people just like you. I have a very full calendar and work by appointment only. Why don't we set aside a specific time just for you—how's tomorrow afternoon at 1:00?"

Whether by phone or in person, if your prospects refuse an appointment, they are telling you they are not seriously interested at this time. Or, if a second or third follow-up appointment is necessary, but they are unwilling to commit, they are, by their lack of commitment, telling you their true priorities. If there is a valid reason and you have a qualified buyer with interest, they will always be open and receptive to additional callbacks and appointments.

STRATEGY #3: Withholding Information by a Controlled Release

Surveys show only a handful of prospects will come back to your sales center and model homes on their own. The psychology and strategy of follow up is that your prospect must have a reason to come back or call back, and the salesperson must have a reason to call back and invite back.

Your company's product literature will undoubtedly include brochures, technical data, audio or video promotional tapes, and a plethora of information at your disposal. You can either place it directly in a prospect's hands, or drop it in the mail as a fulfillment package for those who call for information.

Though all your product information is designed to intrigue a potential customer, the worst mistake you can make is to mail or hand deliver a blizzard of information including every brochure, floor plan and data sheet you can cram into a folder.

You may be uncomfortable with this strategy of withholding information because you may be accustomed to passing out advertising packages. But that is exactly what you don't want to do. You inflict the prospect with information overload. Remember, that 75 percent of all brochures end up in a trash can within 24 to 72 hours.

More importantly, the reason to withhold information and distribute it on a limited basis is that, if you give them all the information at once, you will leave yourself without a reason or an opportunity for continuing conversations and appointments.

In new home and neighborhood sales, there will always be a request for information and, with it, the probability of continuing appointments. The request for information is the perfect reason for another appointment or call.

Perhaps you have a video, brochure, and various other information accessible. If, during your sales conversation, you know you are unable to conclude the sale, then give them a piece of literature. Hand your prospect an overview brochure and say something like, "Miss Prospect, I have an outstanding video presentation that personifies the lifestyle of our community, and I'd love to share it with you. Let's set some time aside when we can get back together and I'll be sure to have the video ready for our next meeting."

To keep your integrity intact and to withhold information on an honest basis, never have any materials preassembled or readily available other than the materials you would use in your presentation. Then, if a prospect asks for product literature, you reply, "I'm happy to provide that information; however, this is my only copy. Allow me the time to customize a brochure package and I'll have it available for our next appointment (or phone conversation)." Then close on the continuing appointment.

If you give all your product information—price sheets, terms, availability, floor plans and renderings—on the first visit, they do not need to see you again. Also, they will use your information to compare your community and homes with the competition's and possibly cross you off the list.

STRATEGY #4: Follow-Up and the Telephone

From a cost-benefit consideration, the telephone is a great communication tool. Letters take time, and with postage and materials, it is estimated that the cost of sending a single letter is somewhere between $5. and $15. Face-to-face calls have been estimated to cost companies well over $250, so obviously from a purely objective point of view, the telephone costs significantly less than either a visit or a letter. Of course, the telephone is less personal than a face-to-face call, but it's more personal than a letter.

The primary disadvantage of the telephone is that you are limited because your voice is the only vehicle carrying your message. Therefore, before attempting your phone conversation, remember that your voice will have to substitute for a firm handshake, your stylish clothing, your friendly smile and other clues visible in face-to-face selling. As a matter of fact, when utilizing the phone, research shows that when people can't see you, your vocal quality, your tonality and delivery account for 80 percent of the believability you have.

Here are two quick tips when using the telephone. First, put a smile in your voice. Do you know it requires 13 facial muscles to smile, while it takes 64 muscles to frown? This means you can work yourself to death without a smile on your face. Tension will be evident in your voice. So smile when you sell—whether it's in person or on the phone.

Second, to transmit high levels of energy, try standing during your conversations. Why? Because you are able to breathe deeply and naturally, and your voice has a better tone. Plus, when you stand, you are literally thinking on your feet and are talking to your prospects and customers much the same as you would face-to-face. Invest in a 25-foot extension cord for your telephone. This will give you plenty of room to move around.

Voice mail does not count

Contact with answering machines and voice mail does not count. Many salespeople view answering machines and voice mail as a blessing with their prospecting and follow up because they do not have to experience rejection.

Picture this. You are at your desk making calls and get an answering machine. You are actually glad you did not have to talk to anyone. After wiping the sweat from your brow and letting out a sigh of relief, you leave a hurried message saying, "Hi, this is Myers. Just wanted to touch base. Call me if you need anything." Leaving messages like this is inactive follow up and is creatively avoiding personal contact and rejection. Answering machines and voice mail do not count in proactive follow up campaigns.

Conversations should be professional

Let me share with you my opinion of what professionalism is. Being a professional isn't determined by the business you are in or the company you represent. Being a professional is determined by the way you conduct yourself in your business.

People know a real professional by his or her telephone etiquette. Therefore, be brief, cordial and to the point in your conversation. Phone rapport should be strictly business and each call must have a specific objective, which is determined prior to making the call.

Many times, when consulting, I'll meet a salesperson who tells me, "I made ten calls today in my prospecting and follow up."

My first question is, "How many people did you talk to?"

"Well, I talked to four, because I got six answering machines or voice mail messages."

My next question is "Did you make a sale or set an appointment?"

"Well, no, but I made my calls." Now, in their defense, they actually achieved their goal, which was to make ten calls.

In an effective follow up campaign, the goal is not making the call. The goal is making the sale, gaining commitment to an appointment, or a continuing conversation. Unless you are setting and achieving specific objectives for your calls, then you are serving more as a social director than as a professional salesperson.

Always obtain a phone number from call-ins

If someone calls in for information to be mailed, always obtain his phone number. It is very frustrating to have someone call for information and then, when you ask for his telephone number, he says, "No, I don't want to give out my number. Just put the information in the mail and I'll call you back after I've had time to review it."

Refer back to Strategy #2. All call backs and contacts in an efficient follow-up campaign are initiated by you. Stay strong on this point! If a caller refuses to give her number, do not waste your time and the company's resources mailing information. Why? Because if she doesn't want to leave her number, then you have no way to follow up, answer questions, obtain an appointment or consummate a sale.

The final point is the most critical. Follow up and confirm your calls by a letter or a fax. Important conversations, such as calls that lead to an appointment, need a letter of confirmation. **A call is just a call. A letter or fax following up a call adds power.**

STRATEGY #5: The Facts About the Fax

One of the greatest ways available today to contact your prospect is via a facsimile. Why? A fax has a sense of priority and importance. People screen and avoid calls and discard their mail, but seem to always read a faxed correspondence. Many professionals and individuals even have home fax machines.

How easy is it to obtain a fax number? Simply include this category on your prospect cards. During your initial discussions, when you are gathering their home addresses and phone numbers, ask for the fax. If you do not have their fax numbers, simply pick up the phone, identify yourself and say, as I do: "Hi, this is Myers Barnes. I have some information I need to fax to Mrs. Prospect. May I have her direct fax number?" To date, I have never been refused a fax number.

Staging the fax campaign

1. Always be conscious of the time of day you send your fax. Be aware that a lot of "junk faxes" are sent by machines overnight. If you send a fax after office hours it could very well be lost in a mountain of other fax transmissions and you stand less of a chance of being noticed.

2. The fax is not a suitable medium for cold-call generation. Sending unsolicited fax messages to people with whom you do not have a relationship is considered rude and inappropriate in many business circles, and may even be illegal in certain jurisdictions. The fax is only to be utilized after an initial contact.

3. Write with a broad tip felt pen or type it on your computer. A standard pen or pencil is often wiped out or erased in transmission. For emphasis, highlight or circle important points with your felt tip pen, or "bold" them on you computer.

4.   A fax, when possible, should not be more than one page. Certainly never more than three or four pages unless, of course, you have a specific request for that much information.

5.   There are two schools of thought regarding cover sheets. You may consider dropping a cover sheet altogether. If you're sending a letter by fax, you probably already have the parties' names on the document. On the other hand, a cover sheet by itself is sometimes enough and a hand-written fax is like a personal note. When you are faxing material that does not have the recipient's name on it, include a cover sheet with the person's name and number of pages when someone other than that individual may receive fax transmissions—as in an office or corporate setting. Always make certain your name, as the sender, is prominent.

6.   Be creative with a fax. For ease of response, you might develop a double fax: send a fax with a space on it for the receiver to simply fill in the information or confirmation and return it to you. This way they can return the same fax without having to write a separate letter.

7.   A fax can issue an ultimatum for a response from prospects who will not return your call. This is my favorite use of a fax. Have you ever called a client six or more times and left messages for a return call on their voice mail or with their secretary and not received a return call? It's frustrating, not to mention inconsiderate.

Realize, when this happens, you are probably being avoided and your prospect is not interested. However, before you give up the ship and discard the prospect completely, issue an ultimatum fax that says, "Miss Prospect, obviously you are as busy as I am. We seem to have a hard time connecting. If you are indeed sincere, simply fax back a convenient time we can speak, or call my office and leave a message with a convenient time." If your prospect has not returned multiple calls and then will not respond to a fax such as this, it's time to press on to a new opportunity.

8. The fax is also a great method to build urgency and gain commitment. Feel free to fax contracts when you are trying to gain an instant decision, and, of course, follow up with hard copies in the mail.

Here are some creative ways to use your fax to stay in contact with your customers and to make your presence known.

- Transmit weather and weekend event information to out-of-state prospects with a "wish you were here" note.

- Transmit updated information on the availability of homes and homesites.

- Announce recent news about your company, or a promotion weekend that's approaching.

- Inform customers about some special interest activities that might pique their interest, such as auctions, open houses, craft shows, art exhibits, wine tastings or festivals. Keep notations current on your customer's hobbies and special areas of interest.

- Send them articles that you have clipped relating to their new home/community.

- Offer Web site updates, with information about changes on your company's Web page or the local Chamber of Commerce's Web site.

- Tell them about a restaurant promotion they might enjoy. Offer to make the reservations.

- Provide current status on the construction of their new home.

- Answer some frequently asked questions, including updates on how sales are going for the week.

Remember you are striving to differentiate yourself from the competition, and build trust and establish confidence with potential customers. Use the fax to confirm your appointments and phone conversations. A follow-up fax immediately after a phone call confirming your discussions and appointments is a guaranteed method to set yourself apart from the competition.

STRATEGY #6: The Mail Follow-Up Campaign

It is essential in a productive follow-up campaign that your prospects see and hear your name countless times. *Your purpose is to build top-of-the-mind awareness.* In advertising, this is called a "saturation campaign" because an area is being flooded with one message.

There is one grave danger with letters as a follow up. Most people read their mail by their wastebasket. Think carefully for just a moment about how you read your personal mail. Is a trash can nearby? Don't you normally scan your mail and quickly determine what you are going to open first? Many letters or packages that are addressed with computer labels and then stamped with a postage meter are thrown into the wastebasket without ever being opened because they are perceived as "junk mail."

Well, your prospects open their mail the same way, so the governing rule is this: If you expect your mail to gain the attention of a prospect, don't send it with a computer label or postage meter. If it's meaningful correspondence, try hand-addressing it in blue ink and put a stamp on it, and your letter should make it through the sea of junk mail and be opened and read.

Here are two additional quick tips that will get your brochures opened. Try the U.S. Postal Service's Priority Mail; the envelope will grab attention. Or, if Priority Mail is not in your budget but you are mailing first class, try first class envelopes rather than using envelopes with a company logo. A first class envelope is classy and clearly marked First Class so it garners the attention your mail deserves.

After insuring that your mail will be opened and read, your next priority is to follow up your letters or brochures with a phone call within two to three days after the prospects have received them. If you are not going to do this, then don't waste your time or company resources mailing information. Mailing information without a follow up call is a creative method that many salespeople employ to avoid personal contacts and experience rejection.

The most efficient way to initiate your call following a letter or fax is to employ a strong call to action at the conclusion of your correspondence. Most letters are concluded with a limp, ineffective ending such as, "If you are interested, please feel free to call," or "I look forward to hearing from you after you have had time to review the information." Ending business correspondence in this way leaves a salesperson hoping for results that probably won't ever materialize.

Instead, conclude your letters with the following call to action: "I will be calling September 24, after you have had time to review the information, for a convenient time to meet." A specific call to action will set up your phone call in advance because now your prospect expects a follow-up conversation. If they know in advance you are going to call, it gives your prospect a deadline to heed in reviewing your letter and brochures. Plus, if a secretary answers your call, you can honestly say, "May I speak with Mrs. Prospect, please? She's expecting my call."

STRATEGY #7: Follow-Up and E-Mail

Rapid advances in technology now allow us to economically and immediately communicate nearly anywhere in the world via electronic mail.

E-mail provides us with diversity, choice, speed, mobility and information. In using it, think creatively. The two elements people want from this form of communication are (1) easy retrieval and, (2) for it to be an enjoyable, rewarding experience.

What *you're* looking for is timeshare. You want your customer to spend as much time with you as prudent, whether it's reviewing material you've electronically mailed to him, speaking to you on the telephone, or talking with you in person.

This is the age of new media and, in the territory of technology, the customer isn't only king, he is Prime Minister, president and controller. He can, with the click of a button, disconnect himself from you. Therefore, it's important that, when using e-mail, you make certain you aren't wasting your customer's time but are making it worth his time.

Used effectively, e-mail can be one of the ways you keep a presence in front of your customer and develop client loyalty. In the mid-nineties, a Bain & Co. study confirmed that if you increase customer loyalty, you'd increase profits. This concept isn't surprising, but the amount of the increase is. The study showed that a five percent increase in loyalty could translate into a 60 percent increase in profitability.

The more contact you have with your customers, the better your chances are of developing that sense of loyalty.

Electronically, you can create your own Web site from which your customers can connect and receive information on such topics as preparing your house to sell, what to look for when buying a new home, decorating tips, etc. This doesn't have to be lengthy—in fact, it's better when downloading your site is fast. These electronic "brochures" you create will to keep your prospects in the buying mood and place your name in front of them. From your Web site, they can easily respond to you by clicking on your e-mail address.

Most of the same rules of etiquette that apply with the fax are applicable to e-mail. Do not cold-call or send unsolicited e-mail to people with whom you have no relationship or who have not requested it. To do so is rude and inappropriate business behavior.

Regardless of which medium you use to communicate with your prospect, a proactive campaign consists of massive and consistent contact and is designed to build awareness and establish you as a professional. Proactive follow up says: A letter or brochure is a trigger for a call; a call is a trigger for a follow-up fax or letter; and all appointments are to be confirmed by fax, letter or calls. With this much contact, do you think a potential customer will perceive you as a results-oriented professional, committed to excellence and service? Of course! And even more importantly, you will set yourself apart in the competitive field of new home and neighborhood sales.

STRATEGY #8: Ranking Prospects

All prospects are not created equal. Your list of prospective buyers requires constant qualification (Chapter 7, Discovery). You cannot afford to waste valuable time by desperately chasing unqualified prospects. Prospects will be ranked by their motivation to purchase in direct correlation to their time frame to purchase. A simple way to do this is to rank your potential customers by the A, B, C method.

An "A" prospect is hot! These prospects are qualified, and have a genuine interest and the need to own. They also have the financial resources and the authority to render a decision. "A" sales leads are those who will own within 30 days.

"B" prospects are warm and are those who will own within 60 days. They are interested, but not in a position to own because of a condition. Remember a condition states one of the areas of qualification cannot be immediately met. Perhaps finances are not available until a later date, or a presentation to all pertinent decision-makers is set for the future. Whatever the condition, you want to initiate a regular follow-up program.

A "C" sales lead is neither hot nor warm. "C" sales leads are normally 90 days to one year into the future. Periodic contact is all that is necessary to keep your name fresh in their minds should their conditions change.

Regarding the A-B-C ranking method, the time frames mentioned (30, 60, or 90 days) are for *example purposes only*. You will need to determine the current sales cycle of your community and set appropriate time frames. Some buying cycles may be a week, while some can be months. Regardless, rank your prospects with the ABC method and validate appropriate time frames, geared to your sales cycle and your prospects' level of qualification.

Now, let's determine the contact frequency—how often and how much contact you maintain with potential customers until a transaction is completed.

STRATEGY #9: Contact Frequency

If "A" sales leads are going to purchase from you or someone else within 30 days, you must posses a bulldog tenacity and be unmerciful with your follow up! I suggest you maintain contact every day or at least every other day.

I know what you're thinking: "But Myers, won't I be bothering them if I contact them every day or every other day?" It's your job to bother them, as long as you are bothering them with solutions to their needs. Realize that if they have a need, and they are going to own, they do not mind having you contact them, as long as your contacts and conversations are centered on satisfying them.

Using the phone, fax, and mail, it is easy to keep your name and community fresh in their minds. If they are going to own a new home or homesite within 30 days, they will do so from the person they perceive is paying attention to their needs. So pay attention!

If "B" sales leads will purchase within 60 to 90 days, contact them every week to ten days. How? Employ Strategy #3 and withhold information, feeding the information to your prospect in a systematic method. Incorporate all you have learned. Make a call, follow up with a fax. Letters, calls, faxes, product literature, and e-mail are all vehicles that allow constant contact.

"C" Sales Leads have no definite time frame for making a purchase. Monthly and quarterly contact to qualified buyers is sufficient. You are simply keeping your name fresh in their minds, building top-of-the-mind awareness for when their time is right.

> NOTE: *With your contact frequency, be sure your follow up is divided between business today versus business in the future. Business today is someone who will own today versus six to eight months in the future. If all of your follow up is for business that is six to eight months in the future, then your results and commissions will be many months away. You don't need that.*

STRATEGY #10: Requalify Your Prospects Monthly as Well as Quarterly

Every month, and certainly every quarter, you should scrutinize and requalify your leads. In doing so, don't be afraid to discard old, unqualified leads.

It's amazing how some salespeople and developers today seem to equate a large list of names with a security blanket. I see some who have hundreds, and sometimes, thousands or more names. They think names equal potential. The more they have, the more they'll sell. So, when they have a large database full of names, they have unlimited potential.

If you were to requalify and scrutinize your list of past prospects, you may end up having to discard the majority. That's good. A security blanket of unqualified prospects who cannot own is not a security blanket at all, but a cement blanket that will weigh you down. They are a major hindrance because you keep contacting and working leads that are never going to materialize into owners. Why do it? You could spend this time working qualified prospects. The bottom line is: If they are not going to own, let them go.

Without fail, this is the one strategy that receives the most controversy when I'm consulting and speaking. Why? Because most people who have hundreds of past leads and names literally fear letting them go. So I'm going to issue you a challenge. You need to perform an acid test on your database. If you see the name of someone you do not recognize and ask yourself, "Who's that?" then realize that's exactly what your prospect will say if you were to call.

If you don't believe this, pick up the phone and call the person. If they do not remember you immediately, be willing to vaporize them from your database.

The most comfortable and effective way to clean out your database is to design a letter with a response mechanism or bounce back card that, in essence, says, "In the past, I have mailed you information you requested. I am currently updating my files. If you are still interested, simply call or mail the enclosed card back, and I will continue to update you. Otherwise, I promise not to bother you again and will remove you from my mailing list."

With a call to action like this, you will find the response overwhelming...overwhelming in that most will not reply. But you're through chasing phantoms and can redirect your energy and resources toward productive prospects.

STRATEGY #11: The Key to Follow Up is Organization, Routine and Habit

Your potential customers are also another salesperson's prospects. Therefore, persistence and consistency in contacting your prospects will build trust and a meaningful business relationship. The moment you stop calling or writing is the moment they may become involved with another salesperson.

Keep current on your follow up. If a prospect tells you to call in 90 days, call back in 30 days. If he says, call back in 30 days, call back in two weeks. Many times the condition that prohibited a buying decision is eliminated before you were instructed to call back. Conditions and motivations change. Your job with follow up is to be in front of your prospect at the moment of change.

STRATEGY #12: Follow Through on Your Promises

Whatever you promise, you must deliver. Sometimes in the exuberance of a sales presentation, we make promises with the best of intentions. We may judge ourselves by our intentions, but our prospects and customers judge us by our actions. The proverb "Actions speak louder than words" is true. Another one states, "What you're doing is so loud I can't hear what you're saying." Your credibility is established or lost based on your performance, not on your good intentions, or what you say you will do.

Promise a letter and don't deliver and you have lost your credibility. If you promise information on Tuesday and deliver on Friday, you will be viewed as unreliable. And, of course, if you are late for an appointment or do not return calls promptly, you appear negligent

199

and send a clear message about yourself and also about the company you represent.

Remember, the purpose of follow up is to build trust, establish a business relationship and maintain the momentum until a transaction is complete. So, in pursuing your prospects, don't make excuses... make good!

15

STEP 9 OF THE POWER PROCESS: FOLLOW THRU — YOU'VE ONLY JUST BEGUN

Long-range planning does not deal with future decisions, but with the future of present decisions

~Peter Drucker

❧   ❧   ❧

If you play golf or tennis, you will easily relate to follow-through. You keep your eye on the ball and follow through with your swing. The same is true in new home and neighborhood sales. After your customer has purchased, he or she enters into the delivery stage. Until your customer takes possession of his or her new home or homesite, you must commit to follow-through with good customer service.

Following through is the sale in progress. It will take you from sale to satisfaction. During that time, the relationship will **intensify and develop further**. Many times, as salespeople, we feel our job is over the moment the customer purchases. When the paperwork is processed, we're ready to dust off our hands and move on to the next opportunity. This type of mentality will destroy any chance of a long-term career in community sales.

The very nature of our business is long term. You aren't selling an item that can be charged, bagged and carried out the door. A single homesite sale can take 30 to 60 days to bring to closure. A complex custom home sale can stretch over what seems like an eternity. You have a long road between your point of sale and final delivery. Countless things can happen to cause the buyer to become dissatisfied and even to lose interest during that time.

Work to keep the relationship going in the right direction. Don't be like the man who pulled his car over to ask a youth on the side of the road how far it was to a certain destination. The youth replied, "If you keep going the way you are headed, it will be about 25,000 miles. But if you turn around, it will be about three miles."

To know where you and your customers are going at all times, you must stay in contact. Otherwise, you might end up on the other side of town wondering what happened.

Anticipating Cancellation

One of the most common reasons for cancellation is the rescission clause that is built into a planned community's sales contract. Yet cancellation isn't necessarily a symptom of the clause. Many times it is, instead, the presentation of the clause.

Widespread debates and philosophical discussions center on whether to present this portion of the contractual agreements to the customer. In my opinion, unless the customer actually questions the existence of the clause, it is an unnecessary discussion between you and your customer. The most profound thought I can offer is: Customers buy what you sell. Sell rescission and they will buy into it, and cancellation will almost be inevitable.

Sometimes there is a belief by inexperienced and desperate sales-people that if you "throw enough stuff against the wall, some of it will stick." Having been a nationwide sales manager and consultant for a number of years, I can personally attest to the fact that many salespeople sell rescission.

Just let the prospect even allude to something like, "What are our chances of backing out at a later date?" Then the desperate salesperson retreats by saying something to the effect of, "Mr. and Mrs. Prospect, not to worry. Our contracts have a built-in clause that addresses that issue. Let's just go ahead for now, and over the next seven days you are protected and can cancel the contract and get your money back. That should give you enough time, won't it?"

That's an interesting script! A sale has just been made. Unfortunately, the sale was rescission.

Again, avoid the discussion of cancellation unless specifically asked. However, many of our buyers know of the rescission clause and may address the issue. If this is the case, my favorite reply is:

Superachiever: "Mr. and Mrs. Prospect, you are correct that most paperwork today includes a clause that allows a period of time to rethink your position. However, that is not my personal policy. As I mentioned before, our rate of sales is ___ new customers joining our community at the rate of ___ new homeowners per week. It's unfair to potential customers, as well as my team members and company, to make this premier property unavailable for even a brief period of time. I don't think it is in your best interest to proceed forward under that type of premise. Obviously, you have concerns that I have not properly addressed. Before moving forward, let's discuss your last minute questions and concerns."

You have just presented what is probably the boldest "take away" close you could give a customer. However, if you will be courageous, you will find in most cases the customer will proceed forward. Should you retreat and sell rescission, realize that you have completely diminished your urgency and devalued the property. *After all*, if the homes and homesites in your community are in such demand (as you should have been conveying throughout the sales process with a strong sense of urgency), why would you be willing to take such a valuable piece of property off the market?

It's the Next Day. Do You Know Where Your Customers Are?

The most common reason a sale will fall apart is "buyers remorse." The new home or homesite sale is a significant and emotional experience, and indecision and doubts will many times begin to emerge even before the ink has dried. This occurs after the customer leaves your presence, and the impact of what they have done begins to "hit home." In the car or at home, they begin to mentally replay all their concerns. The problem is now they are alone and you are not present to answer their renewed objections and concerns.

Many times, when left alone, they will seek the advice of a third party. During this stage, the buyer may talk with a relative, friend or counselor and, without fail, the armchair response is usually, "You did what?" The customer's newly adopted sales consultant loves his or her role and sometimes makes a negative comment about the purchase because of ego or envy. Maybe these "crackerjack consultants" are jealous to see their friends owning something new, or maybe they want a new home but can't afford one themselves. Regardless, your customer is now under pressure to justify his decision.

To prevent this, you must reassure your customers that they can call you anytime with questions or concerns, and you must call them and do a "reality check" to confirm that they are still happy homeowners.

Have you ever received the call or letter canceling the purchase a few days later or maybe just hours prior to the expiration of a revocation clause? It would be my guess that cancellation did not occur over the course of days, but within hours. They just wait a few days before notifying you.

Sometimes it is wise to withhold a piece of information, such as a brochure or handout. That allows you to revisit them later in the day or that evening. And it is important that the visit occur that very day as opposed to the next day. If there is anguish, they will spend a sleepless night, and the majority of the decision to cancel may be reached prior to the next day.

You could withhold hard copies of the contractual agreements, offering to deliver them that evening. Or, you could drop by with a simple gift, such as a bottle of wine or bouquet of flowers. The reason for the visit is unimportant. This just allows you a valid excuse to see them to address any remaining questions and concerns.

A strategy my friend Bill employs is to send the customers to dinner the evening of their purchase as his guest. He first calls for the reservation at a restaurant of his choice. Then he instructs them to deliver the bill to him the next day or he will swing by to deliver a check to repay them. This gives him a reason to contact his customers that evening to inquire about their dining experience, but more importantly to answer any lingering concerns. And the next day he or his personal assistant will again see the customers in person to solidify the sale.

Facilitating the Details

Whoever said "No news is good news" was not a part of the profession of new community and neighborhood sales. If you ever want a sale or business relationship to unravel, forget who your customer is after they buy but before they take delivery. If difficulties should occur during the delivery stage, you must be the one keeping your customer informed. You, the salesperson, initiated the business relationship and it should be sustained by you. As best you can, anticipate and eliminate all those armchair consultants before they have an opportunity to ambush your customers.

Most sales are made subject to financing and mortgage approval. Therefore, it should be mentioned that this in itself can be an easy escape clause if buyers want to unqualify themselves through the information they provide, or refuse to provide, to the lender. It is important for you to realize that, during the mortgage process, the buyer may still be experiencing mental justification. Therefore, it is your job to facilitate the details of the actual meeting between loan officer and customer and the series of actions directed toward financial approval.

Unless a buyer has been prequalified prior to purchasing, you cannot let mortgage approval be left to chance. Initially, a customer may want to shop the interest rates. This is dangerous because the lowest rates are not necessarily an indication of the level of professional services rendered by a mortgage company. If the mortgage approval process is challenging, the sale can break apart.

The builder/developer and, more importantly, the salesperson should have a prearranged relationship with a lender or lenders who are not just familiar with the neighborhood but who actually serve as cheerleaders. Remember third party approval? The first person they may choose to see is a lender. Although the loan officer may not intentionally make a detrimental comment, he or she may present a twist that contradicts the salesperson's presentation. Therefore, it would be in yours and your client's best interest to form a quality relationship with a lender who "sings from the same hymnal" and is dedicated to your success.

After forming the relationship, make sure *you* schedule the initial appointment between the loan officer and your customer. And, if necessary, go with your customer for the initial meeting. Without a concrete appointment, the customer may wander off track and visit or call another financial institution. Remember the story of the man asking directions? Well, without your direction, your customer may end up taking the 25,000-mile journey instead of the three-mile journey back to home base.

If you are hesitant about selecting the bank or mortgage company that you determine is best for the customer, then you must shift your thought process. If your customer trusts you, as well as the advice and service you have rendered, to this point in the sale, he will gladly welcome your further assistance and recommendations.

Facilitating the details goes well beyond connecting with the lender. There is the closing attorney, those in your design centers, and a host of others involved in bringing your sale to completion. So stay involved. You aren't just making a sale; you're building a business relationship based on results.

Continuing Follow Through

Victor Hugo said, "He who every morning plans the transactions of the day and follows out that plan carries a thread that will guide him through the labyrinth of the most busy life. The orderly arrangement of his time is like a ray of life, which darts itself through all his occupations. But where no plan is laid, where the disposal of time is surrendered merely to the chance of incident, chaos will soon reign."

You don't need chaos before closing. Therefore, it is important that you schedule your daily and weekly activities to include a regular process of follow through. You need constant contact with the buyer to maintain a satisfactory relationship. At the least, you should have a weekly contact during the preclosing period letting any tidbit of information serve as a reason for the contact.

If your sale includes a new home, you must continue the follow through until delivery occurs. As a salesperson, you have no authority over production schedules. However, this does not make it impossible to check production schedules and keep the customer updated on the sequence of events.

One of the best methods of keeping customers abreast of the construction of their new homes is with photographs. From the beginning of the foundation to the completion of the home, take a weekly photo of the construction process. Have duplicates made. One photo you drop in the mail and the other you save to assemble in a scrapbook. Depending on your construction time line, this could provide you with 20 or more pictorial contacts. It shows the customer your high level of service while they wait. When they move in and receive their completed scrapbook, you have created a customer for life.

In conclusion, sales will go smoother if you: Know where you are going, take your customer with you, plan the journey, and celebrate when you arrive.

16

STEP 10 OF THE POWER PROCESS: REFERRALS—YOU ARE THE MARKETING DEPARTMENT

A customer who purchased once is not a monumental accomplishment. A customer who does business with you a second time, or refers their friends, is a confirmation they like how you do business.
~ **Nido Qubein**

When asked the purpose of business, most entrepreneurs respond: 'To make a profit.' This is true, but it's more than money. The initial purpose of business is to create a customer first; to establish a relationship that will last. Once that's done, the profit will follow.
~ **Myers Barnes**

The customer is king. He, above anyone else, is your boss. Every working person from the president of the corporation to the shoeshine boy has the same boss. He is the customer. He is the one boss you must please. Everything you have ever owned, he has paid for. He buys your home, your cars, your clothing. He pays for your vacations. He writes every paycheck you receive and gives you your promotions. And he will discharge you if you displease him.
~ **Earl Nightingale**

     ❦   ❦   ❦

Results depend on relationships. It is your customer who pays your wages. So it stands to reason that, the more buyers you have, the more money you make.

It sounds logical, but many salespeople have not firmly grasped that singular truth. If they have, they will do everything possible to keep their clients happy and to bring their prospects to closing.

There are two methods you can use to increase your business in the profession of new home and neighborhood sales. You can wait for company-generated walk-in traffic, or you can obtain more business from your existing customers.

The more profitable of the two is to obtain more business from your existing customer base. Every customer is a source of new business and referrals. Once you have satisfied a customer, he or she will continue doing business with you if you follow up and stay in touch.

Customers Buy "More of the Same"

How will customers continue to do business with you? They will eventually purchase another new home or some investment property and you are able to continue to upgrade them in perpetuity if you make them feel like royalty.

Regardless of what was initially purchased (home, homesite or investment property), there will come a time when your customers will become dissatisfied with what they have. Or their investment strategy will change and they will want to upgrade or add to their original investments.

If you engage in good follow through and continue to follow up by maintaining the business relationship, it will be effortless to resell your existing customers, because they have already purchased once. They have done their homework and are familiar with your company and its homes and neighborhoods. But more importantly they trust you, because you have proven yourself to be a professional who anticipates and accommodates their needs.

But, despite this, don't lose sight of the fact that customers are fickle. Whenever there is a need, they expect that need to be satisfied by whomever is paying attention to them. If you do not continuously cultivate customers, someone else will.

Customers Provide Referrals

In addition to buying more property themselves, your customers will also provide you with referrals. What's great about a referral? Referencing the studies quoted in earlier chapters, 68 percent of the decision to purchase is based on the trust and credibility customers feel for the salesperson. As we have discussed, they buy you first before they choose the neighborhood and home. This means a referral prospect is almost 70 percent sold on your personal credibility because someone he or she trusts has recommended you.

Also, for the most part, referrals are prequalified. Are you familiar with the term "nest factor?" It states, "Birds of a feather flock together." If your customers are financially qualified to own, they are, in all probability, associating with and referring to you qualified prospects.

What's the Outcome—The Welfare Line?

If the benefit of referral prospects isn't enough to excite you, then you need to ask yourself the sobering question, "What's the outcome if I do not obtain referrals?"

The outcome is to wait for walk-ins. What's the result of doing this? Well, waiting for walk-ins is like being on welfare.

That's right, waiting for walk-ins, call-ins and company-generated traffic is like being on welfare. You become dependent on the system, which is your company's marketing department. Depending on the system causes you to sit around, day in and day out, saying to your company, yourself and, more importantly, your family, "I don't need help. I need a handout." When business is slow, the cry is always the same: "The marketing programs aren't working," and "Traffic is off."

Pulling yourself off the welfare line starts with your perception of a sale. Most salespeople view the original sales transaction as just a single transaction; whereas the Superachiever views a sale as three potential transactions. The first one is, of course, the original sale. The second transaction occurs when customers eventually own another home or homesite. And the third transaction is in the form of an owner referral. This simple paradigm shift embodies the mindset that a sale is not just a sale, but is actually three sales wrapped into one.

Your goal with referrals should have you setting a minimum standard of "one for one." For every one sale, you will obtain a referral sale. Think of the advantages if you just obtained one referral sale from each customer. Regardless of the number of transactions you have in a year, you would have in your sales funnel the same number of transactions waiting for you the following year. The benefit is that you will never have to start a New Year from ground zero. Couple your referral sales with company-generated sales and your business grows exponentially.

Using referrals makes you proactively in charge of your destiny and allows you the freedom to run your own business completely independent of the marketing department. Notice I said running your business. Do you know what the difference is between running and ruining your business? The letter "I."

When you take charge of your business, which translates into taking charge of your future, you make it happen. Of course, you'll also make mistakes, but even mistakes can work in your favor when you're the one calling the shots.

Campbell Soup's marketing department used to advertise that the company produced 21 different kinds of soup, and listed them. Customers noticed a mistake and pointed out that the list actually contained 22 different soups. Executives of the company met and, instead of correcting the mistake, decided to use it to their benefit when they noticed that as many as 700 people had called or written to the company about the discrepancy. They did not correct the mistake because they said it caused the ads, and their product, to be talked about and provided them with feedback.

Smart business people learn from their mistakes and keep going and growing. They know success is never final and failure's never fatal.

METHODS AND STRATEGIES TO MAINTAIN CUSTOMER CONTACT

Maintaining customer contact starts the day of possession, on the delivery of their new home or homesite. That very day it is appropriate to welcome your customers to their neighborhood with a gift. If it's impossible to meet them personally, then forward the gift, and follow up with a call.

To continue the relationship, small gifts after the delivery and possession date are also appropriate. Gifts do not have to cost a fortune. They need only to express to your customers that you are thinking of them. You can give a gift that relates to your community or area, such as a book of history or architecture, or one about your company, or give one of the country club's polo shirts and hats, or a gift certificate. If your county or city has a weekly newspaper, you can give a one-year subscription. That reminds them of you 52 times that year. Be sure to drop the gift off personally and, so they'll know you are only there momentarily, you can leave your car running and simply say, "I just wanted to give you this gift and tell you how much I appreciate you."

Carry a Camera

Buy a camera and carry it in your car. If you have absentee owners, mail them pictures of wildlife or the change of seasons that you have taken. Absentee owners, as well as local residents, appreciate pictures of their homes or surrounding property under construction. You can take pictures of a golf course under construction or any amenity underway. It's an inexpensive but effective pictorial follow up to have multiple copies of the same pictures run off and mailed to different customers. If you don't want to incur the cost of envelopes, customize a postcard by simply addressing the back of the picture with a Sharpie pen and affixing a stamp. Check with the post office first to make certain it falls within the allowable size for a self-mailer.

Contact Customers on Holidays

Cards are a meaningful contact. However, a once-a-year Christmas card gains no respect and is lost in the shuffle of all the others. A more effective strategy is to contact customers with nontraditional holiday cards. There are companies that manufacture Labor Day, Memorial Day, Groundhog Day, Thanksgiving, Easter, and even Halloween cards. And, of course, there is the most special occasion, each customer's birthday. Had they not been born, you would not have made the sale and they would not be the happy owners of a new home. That's certainly a reason to celebrate.

Contact Customers Whenever There are New Developments and Changes

The release of a new phase, a new neighborhood, or housing lines, with presale information is not only a proactive contact, but just may be the prompting for an additional sale. A little note like, "We're expanding. Do you have some friends you want as neighbors? Now's the time for them to own," might prompt them to offer you some referral names.

Contact Customers with a Personal Newsletter and Newspaper Clippings

A monthly or quarterly newsletter is just smart business and allows mass contact. Also, many times your neighborhood or builder/developer may receive complimentary publicity in a newspaper or publication. Make copies and mail them with a personal note. This is another powerful way to contact your entire customer (and prospect) base in one sweeping motion.

Contact Them on the Anniversary Dates of Their Purchase

You are touching base with your customers to be sure everything is all right, and letting them know you are always available. Literally with holidays, special events and your company's new products, you can easily stay in front of your customers on a monthly, or at least a bimonthly, basis.

You may be thinking, "I have a hundred customers—I can't keep up." Sure you can, if you break it down to its smallest component. A hundred customers over a 20-day work month are only five contacts per day. Of course, if you wait until the end of the month and try to contact 100 customers at one time, you will be overwhelmed. But, if you break it down, commit and allocate twenty to thirty minutes a day to customer follow up, it's possible and profitable to maintain contact.

Realtor and Sphere of Influence Referrals

The days of simply showing up at your model or sales center and picking up a check while waiting for walk-ins are over. It's a new age, and this is one of self-prospecting. Great opportunities await the new home and neighborhood sales Superachiever who takes advantage of networking.

The key to building a Realtor referral business is to understand the Realtor's prospect is not your customer. The Realtors themselves are your customers and they should be respected accordingly. Just like any other customer, the more the Realtor trusts you, the more prospects they will refer to you.

Of course, the natural inclination is to simply shove a card and brochures in a broker's hands and say something to the effect, "If you know anybody who's interested, call me." This ineffective method of prospecting almost insures a nonsuccessful brokerage relationship.

Your first priority should be to visit a realty company office to deliver a presentation during their sales meeting. In this meeting, you will field and answer questions about how you ease the process of working together. Explain how you act as their "personal assistant," and that your top priority is to offer assurances that their customers and commissions are protected with your written guarantee policies.

Although a group meeting is effective, a singular relationship is always best. Maximize your efforts by developing a Top 10 List. The criteria necessary to be included on your Top Realtor List are simple. You add only those cobrokers who *actually sell in the area of your community*. The next stipulation is to focus on Realtors who specialize in selling versus listing. General brokerage is becoming segmented, and many Realtors specialize in either listing properties or solely in selling properties. If a Realtor is number one in her office, but achieves her results by specializing in listings, she is not the candidate you seek. Make sure your efforts are focused on the "area" and "selling specialist." Remember to treat your Top 10 List as your customers, so the strategies for contacting them are the same.

Sphere of Influence Referrals

Who are you helping who can help you? Bankers, closing attorneys and those partners close to your business should feel comfortable in establishing a mutually beneficial relationship. Partnering with others is the embodiment of networking.

Going beyond owners, realtors and partners, make a list of all the people who are significant in your life. Relatives, people in your church or health club, business associates, club members—make them all aware that you are in the business of new neighborhood and home sales. You cannot assume, for even a moment, that everyone in your sphere of influence thinks of you all the time. Keep your "homing devices" constantly tuned for opportunities that come along through other people.

There is no such thing as downtime in new neighborhood and home sales. There is only quiet time while waiting for walk-in traffic. If you want more sales, there is a way of self-prospecting. With you at the helm of your personal marketing department, you can create your own great year.

Referral Prospecting Close

The optimum time to obtain referrals is either immediately after the purchase or at the time of delivery. If you have provided excellent customer service and maintained customer follow up, your customer may provide you with referrals. However, for the most part, you must be willing to ask for them.

Superachiever: "Mr. and Mrs. Customer, I have a favor to ask you."

Customer: "Sure, what is it?"

Superachiever: "With my business, my most valued resource is the customer. My top priority is knowing you are satisfied. You are satisfied and comfortable with your investment decision, aren't you?"

Customer: "We certainly are."

Superachiever: "Then, the favor I ask is this: I would like to share the same opportunity with your friends or relatives. Do two to three persons come to mind who would enjoy the same benefits as you?"

> NOTE: *You have asked for referrals that come to mind immediately with the Alternatives Method. Normally they will choose two because it's easier than naming three.*

After you obtain the names, ask for the phone numbers and, if the customer is extremely comfortable with you, ask that he call ahead to introduce you, your company and services.

Another method for referral prospecting comes from a friend of mine in the insurance business. This is how he asks for referrals:

Superachiever: "Mr. Customer, if your best friends were present right now, would you introduce us to one another?"

Customer: "Certainly, I'd be glad to."

Superachiever: "Mr. Customer, that's exactly what I'd like to ask you to do. Would you mind if I called to introduce myself and my service to two or three of your best friends?"

There is one final method to the Referral Prospecting Close and that is to obtain prospects from people who did not buy. Julie, an outstanding salesperson, always asks for referrals from nonbuyers in the following fashion:

Superachiever: "Mr. Prospect, I understand the timing is not right to own now (or I understand you are not in a position to become involved, or I understand you are not in a position to decide today), but could you give me the names of two or three people you think may be able to take advantage of my services?"

217

Remember that you earn referrals by excellent service. If you have followed through and satisfied the customer with good service and positive results, you have earned the right to ask for referrals.

17

ADVANCED SELLING SKILLS: NEGOTIATION

In negotiating, it's important to practice the art of discretion, which simply means raising your eyebrow instead of your voice.
~ **Myers Barnes**

You have not converted a man because you have silenced him.
~ **John Morley**

⌁   ⌁   ⌁

It is a misconception that, in the case of a new home or homesite, customers are only concerned with the lowest price. Many sales-people and builders/developers think this is so. As a professional, you must realize customers are concerned with more than price, even though you hear them ask "How much per square foot?" when you haven't even had a chance to fully present your neighborhood and homes. That question appearing early in the presentation is just as frustrating as the prospect's responses: "What's the best you will do?" or "Will you take less than the listed price?" or "We can't go over a certain amount," or the classic, "Your competition is cheaper."

As with many objections, the concern about price is predictable. Your prospects and customers will always want to know, "What's the best you will do?" And once you tell them, they often complain. When you realize price resistance is a natural, predictable objection, you are on the way to the top of your profession. Realize, too, that when your customers talk price, they are really wanting you to justify your home's value to them.

THE BASICS OF PRICE RESISTANCE

- **It always costs too much:** A price objection is an automatic response. Everybody asks how much it is and then flinches at the price. All customers, yourself included, become intoxicated with the idea of obtaining the best price possible. Regardless of the cost, their initial reaction is, "It's more than we wanted to pay."

- **Price is the common denominator:** Why does price come up early in the sales presentation? Because it represents something we all have in common—the concern with money. We all relate to dollars and cents.

- **Are they objecting to the price or are you?** For the sales professional, this must be clear. Often the price objection appears in the salesperson's mind first. If you have issue with your neighborhood values, then you won't be able to overcome the objection if your prospect voices it.

Others are always selling their homes or homesites for less. Any low-level order taker can give away his or her homes, upgrades and services at a lower price. The sign of the Superachiever is that he or she can represent the neighborhood values at the one true price, which is the stated value.

THE FOUR PHASES OF NEGOTIATION

1. RELATE: Before you begin to negotiate, you must first establish if your counter party sincerely wants to own a new home or homesite. This is the beginning of building a relationship. It establishes a context in which customers feel comfortable sharing information. As they do, you can determine their levels of commitment.

2. EXPLORE: This can be more time-consuming than you might think. Frequently you must navigate past problems and positions and merge into the reasons they are reluctant to move ahead.

Verbal offers are a worthless sign of commitment. **Commitment comes in the form of a check and a contract.** Unless you have a check and a contract, you are merely having a conversation. If prospects are hesitant to issue that check, continue exploring until you find out where their minds are and what is prompting this reluctance.

3. PROPOSE: In most real estate transactions, the prospect wants to negotiate based on tradition. The tradition is based on your propositions or how you present the contracts.

If your contracts say "Offer to Purchase," change them. Avoid using the following phrases:

"Let's make an offer." or "You will never know unless we ask."

"By law I'm obligated to present any and all offers."

"This home is listed at $___." or "The price they are asking is $___."

4. AGREEMENT: You arrive at an agreement by working through the written proposal one provision at a time, by answering the customers' questions and allaying their fears, and by showing that you truly do have their best interests in mind by helping them find the homes of their choice.

THE FUNDAMENTALS OF NEGOTIATION

1. **Never allude that there may be room to negotiate.** If you are working for the seller (builder or developer), by law you are representing their best interests. *You are not a buyer's agent and the moment you negotiate for the buyer you have crossed the line.*

2. **If you must make concessions, only negotiate terms, conditions, closing dates, initial investment, etc.** *Never the price.*

3. **Negotiation is a mindset.** If you believe in the value of the offer, you will stay strong.

4. **Both sides want something.** You want them to become owners and they want to own a home/homesite. There is equal pressure and you should never approach the negotiation table feeling you are the only one in need. Both parties desire a

specific outcome or there would be no reason to conduct the negotiation.

DEVELOPING NEGOTIATION POWER

Before covering the tactics, there are antecedents to negotiating that must be understood.

The first is **emotion**. The more you are able to keep your emotions out of the negotiations, the better you perform. The key is not to get so caught up that you become overwrought.

Secondly, always appear as a reluctant seller. Perhaps one of the worst mistakes in negotiating is to give away your position when you become anxious, and appear to want what the other party is offering too much. The person who wants it the least, gets the most; or better yet, those who *appear* as though they want it the least, get the most.

Finally, by controlling emotions and appearing as a reluctant seller, the skilled negotiator possesses **"walk away"** power. This means you must decide in advance that you are willing to walk away from the negotiation table all together.

If you ever feel so caught up emotionally that you are willing to give or take what the prospect offers, regardless of cost, you are not in a position to effectively negotiate.

NEGOTIATION TACTICS

The purpose of a tactic is to cause the other person to move from his or her position without moving from your position. As a professional negotiator, tactics must be memorized not only to learn their applications, but also to learn how to deflect a tactic when it is used against you.

Establishing the Strategy

Prospect: "We want to make an offer." or "What's the bottom line?" or "Do you think they will take less?" or "What's the best you'll do?" etc.

NOTE: *Your strategy begins by gaining the customer's commitment that he really wants to own the home or homesite.*

Superachiever: "Are you saying you like this home/homesite and want to own it?" or "Am I understanding you correctly? This is the home/homesite you want to own?"

In the event the prospect responds "No" to your first question, there is no sense in proceeding further with the discussion of price. If that happens, flinch and respond curiously with:

Superachiever: "Really! Why not?"

Do not continue the negotiating process without your customer's confirmation that he sincerely wants to be a homeowner.

❦   ❦   ❦

1. Will You Take Less Than the Listed Price?

Prospect: "We would like to make an offer," or "Will you take less than the listed price?" or "What's the best you can do?" or "What's the bottom line?"

Superachiever: "Are you saying you like this home/homesite and would like to own it?"

Prospect: "Yes, but only if we can get it at the right price" or "at a deal."

Superachiever: "Mr. Prospect, let me ask you this. When you move into your new home and meet your neighbor who says, 'How much of a discount did you get?' or 'What kind of deal did you get?' how are you going to feel? The reality is if we offered discounts to everyone, your neighbor might look at you and say, 'Is that all?' At this point, how would you really feel? I sense now you understand why we don't negotiate. Everyone who owns in ____ gets the same great value. After all, that's what's really important, isn't it?"

Prospect: "I'm only concerned about the deal *I* get. If my neighbors get a better price, then good for them," or "I've never paid full price for real estate."

Superachiever: "I'm curious. Are you familiar with how real estate's true value is determined? In reality, the developer/builder, or the salesperson representing the home/homesite, does not determine value. Value is based on comparable sales. In other words, a professional appraiser says property is only worth the last price for which a home was purchased. If yesterday, someone purchased a comparable home/homesite at $___, and today, you purchase it at $___, then what is the true value? Mr. Prospect, we offer value protection and feel everyone should pay the same fair price. Wouldn't you agree?"

෨෧   ෨෧   ෨෧

2. We Can't Go Over a Certain Amount

Prospects may try to negotiate to further justify their offers by presenting you a fixed amount. Your strategy is to discover how they arrived at their figures.

Prospect: "We can't go over $___."

Superachiever: "Really? I'm curious. How did you arrive at that amount?"

Prospect: "We have been prequalified by the bank."

Superachiever: "What bank prequalified you?" or "On what plan or rate was that based?"

Let them elaborate so you can determine they have indeed been to the bank. If you find this is true, then proceed with Script 1, pages 223, 224.

In the event they haven't been to the bank, they may respond with:

Prospect: "Actually, we aren't sure." or "It's just what we feel we can afford."

Superachiever: "Mr. and Mrs. Prospect, why don't we take a moment to discuss the financing programs available." or "Let's call now and schedule a meeting with the bank to determine the amount they say you may qualify for and the financing opportunities available."

You can then proceed with preparing the contracts, subject to a bank's qualifications.

  ⁊   ⁊   ⁊

3. We Could Have Bought (Months/Years) Ago for a Lot Less Money

Your strategy is to help them discover that their failure to act in the past will only cost more in the future.

Prospect: "We could have bought the same property for $___ last month/year."

Superachiever: "You are not going to let that happen again, are you?"

(If they say no, proceed to contracts. If they hesitate, proceed with the following script:)

Superachiever: "There are only two things that will occur with future real estate values: **price** and **availability**. First, whatever you are looking at today probably will not be available tomorrow, and secondly, you can in all probability, count on the **value increasing**."

"What's important is not to focus on what you could have done in the past, but on what you will do in the future. Let's go ahead and secure your home/homesite today, and next month/year you can sit back and realize you received today's best value in the time frame that was perfect for you."

  ⁊   ⁊   ⁊

4. Negotiating with a "Buyer's Agent"

When a buyer's broker is negotiating on a customer's behalf, the strategy is to make sure the broker understands why you do not negotiate price.

Superachiever: "Miss Broker, let me explain why we do not negotiate price. There are primarily two reasons: First, I don't have to tell you about comparable sales. Any time we cut prices, we depreciate the values in the neighborhood."

"You have access to the local MLS and can see everyone paid the same fair price, which is the stated value. We've promised our customers value protection. Don't you think your customer wants to invest in a community where the developer/builder is committed to the homeowner's best interest?"

"Also, what if, after your customers move in, they meet their neighbors who say to them, 'How much of a discount did your Broker negotiate?' The reality is, this may happen. So how do you think your customers would feel if they discovered another broker had negotiated a better price or concession than you?"

"I sense you now understand why we will not place you in a compromising situation. Everyone gets the same great value and we are building long-term relationships with professionals such as you. It's in everybody's best interest, don't you think?"

5. The Customer Insists on Presenting a Written Offer

When the customer firmly demands a written offer and you are forced to write the agreement for anything less than full price, then be sure to state to them the following:

Superachiever: "Mr. Prospect, I appreciate your position and understand you just want assurances that this home/homesite is being presented at the best value available. I just want you to understand this is out of the ordinary and I feel certain it will not be accepted as it is written. With that in mind, do you still want me to present this offer?"

Prospect: "Let's see what happens." or "We won't know unless we try."

Very important: The rule is that you negotiate terms and conditions—never price. You may negotiate:

- Closing date

- Initial investment

- Upgrade or options to the home/homesite

    NOTE: *Never present a counteroffer over the telephone. If possible, always present the counteroffer face-to-face. Set a concrete appointment prior to leaving, or phone the prospect to make a person-to-person appointment.*

Superachiever: "This is the best I can do and as far as my company can go. I am not able to offer any further concessions. I sense you really want this home, is that right?"

Prospect: "Yes, but I've never paid full price for real estate."

Superachiever: "I understand, and at the same time it's unfortunate we cannot put this together today, because the moment I walk out, your home/homesite will be made available to someone else." (Pause for reaction or response, then continue.)

"Mr. Prospect, is it just a matter of principle, or are you short $___, the difference in the amount about which we are talking?"

If they have the money, and so acknowledge, say, "Congratulations on your new home." If they do not, then present a note for the amount of the difference due 30, 60 or 90 days and/or negotiate terms and conditions.

∽   ∽   ∽

6. The Competition Will Discount Their Homes

This strategy is two-fold requiring two strategies. In the first script, ask the prospect why they haven't purchased. Though this is a bold response, if it was a "deal," they would not be talking to you. In the second script, you want them to realize someone else's deal may not be to their true advantage.

Prospect: "Your competition is making better deals," or "...will cut their prices," or "...is offering substantial incentives."

Superachiever: ""Mr. Prospect, I do not want to appear discourteous, but I'm puzzled. If you felt it's such a great price, why haven't you purchased one of their homes?"

Remain silent and let them state their reasons: They might like the homes but not the community, or they like the price, but not the designs, quality, etc.

Superachiever: "Mr. Prospect, it seems price is not the true issue. What you're really concerned with is obtaining the best value, is that correct? Let's take a moment to discuss what's truly the best value for your family and/or investment needs."

Prospect: "Your competition has a better deal," or ..."will discount their prices."

Superachiever: "I don't understand their business strategy! Mr. and Mrs. Prospect, why do you think they would do that?"

Prospect: "They are having a difficult time selling homes," or "They want to sell homes," or "I don't care/know why, but they are."

Superachiever: "Are you comfortable with the thought that they are cutting prices/deals? I'm just a little concerned. Will you ever know if you got the best price or did someone else get a better deal than you did? And if they are having a difficult time selling homes, will you be comfortable making the single largest investment of your life with a community/builder who is having a difficult time selling homes?"

Prospect: "I haven't really given it much thought," or "You may be right."

Superachiever: "There are a lot of ways to cut corners and prices when building a home. Like you, I really don't know what's going on, but I can assure you our commitment is to long-term customer service and to giving you the best value available. Let's take a few moments and talk about the *best value for the single largest investment of your life.*"

❧   ❧   ❧

7. We Can Get a Better Price Per Square Foot

The prospect may try to negotiate by comparing your price per-square-foot with another builder.

Superachiever: "We have never looked at it that way. You see, there are so many variables—materials, warranties, and customer satisfaction—when determining the price of a home. I'm curious. Are you looking for your new home based solely on price per-square-foot?"

Prospect: "No, but we do want the best price."

Superachiever: "Great, then what you're looking for is the best value, is that correct?"

Superachiever: "Determining a square-foot-price is difficult, as a home's true value is not determined by square footage, but by component parts, such as the materials in the home. Let me give you an example. The price of carpet is $____per square yard, while tile is $____per square foot. We need to determine what you would like in your home and then price the home according to the materials we use. That makes sense, doesn't it?"

Superachiever: "In searching for a new home, there are three points to consider: 1) Price per square foot 2) Quality and 3) Service. Unfortunately, as a builder/developer, we can only deliver two of the three at the same time. Which two are you most interested in receiving?"

❧   ❧   ❧

8. We Can Buy a Bigger/Larger Home From the Competition

The prospect may try to negotiate by stating the competition builds larger homes, with less custom features than yours.

Superachiever: "Mr. and Mrs. Prospect, we don't just build a big box with a lot of square footage at the cheapest price. Our commitment is to design and customize features that reflect your personal taste, to make your home as unique as your personal signature. We pay attention to craftsmanship, quality materials and life-long commitment to customer satisfaction. All things considered, if you base your decision on price-per-square-foot and a big box is what you want, we may not have what you're seeking. Now that you understand our value is in the total package, can we take a few moments to discuss what features are important to you/your family?"

Superachiever: "Mrs. Prospect, the big basic box you are considering may be an outdated plan. Let me explain. Ten years from now when you want to sell your home, if your floor plan is ten years old, then you are really marketing a 20-year-old home. Our designs are cutting edge, up-to-date and will carry forward, holding their value for years to come when it is time to resell."

"There are a lot of ways to cut price when building a home and constructing a big box is one way, but it is not forward thinking in this day and age. Let's discuss and review those plans that are a reflection of your personal taste, but will still retain their value in the future."

By negotiating with your customers, you help them solidify their home-buying goals. The next chapter will help you focus on your own goals.

18

GOALS:
TAKING CHARGE OF YOUR
DESTINY

*Your problem is to bridge the gap that exists between
where you are now and the goal you intend to reach.*

~ **Earl Nightingale**

*If you don't know where you're going, every road will get
you nowhere.*

~ **Henry Kissinger**

A pioneer is not defined so much as a person in time, but as a person in spirit. Do you have the pioneer spirit? Are you ready to explore new territory? Is it time for you to set new goals and head in a different direction? Are you ready for change and to go forward in your life?

Before you begin, you need to map out the territory; decide where you are and where you want to be. When you are making changes, whether those changes or internal or external, long-range goals will keep you from being frustrated with short-term failures.

Having a goal gives you direction. Goals reflect your purpose in life and let you know if you're on target. When an archer misses the mark, he turns and looks within himself for the fault. Failure to hit the bull's eye is never the fault of the target. To improve your aim, improve yourself.

Intensely focused goal planning is the essential characteristic of all high-achieving men and women in every field, in every instance, in every study.

THE YALE STUDY

In 1953, the graduating class of Yale University was interviewed and asked, "Do you have a specific written plan of action (goals) for your life?" Three percent of the class had committed, in writing, the goals for their lives following a specific procedure that will be described in this chapter. That meant ninety-seven percent of the class, though well educated, would be going into the world traveling by the seat of their pants and winging it.

Twenty years later, in 1973, the class was again interviewed, and the study revealed that the three percent who had established a clearly written, detailed plan for their lives had accumulated more wealth than the other ninety-seven percent combined. In addition, the three percent with goals were happier, better adjusted, and much more excited about life in general.

Suppose you were taken out to sea thirty miles from shore in a marvelous sailing vessel. Once on the water, your ship is stripped of its sails, rudder, compass, backup engines and radio communication equipment. How will you now get home? On what are you totally dependent?

Like a piece of wood, you will aimlessly drift and float, dependent upon the tides. A person without goals is like a ship without a rudder, adrift without a captain or destination, floating aimlessly through life with little hope of finding a harbor.

Or suppose you were on a nonstop flight to the Orient and heard this announcement: "Ladies and gentlemen, this is your captain speaking. We're traveling west across the Pacific Ocean. In a few hours, you will be able to look down and see land. When that happens, we're going to start looking for a big city with an airport.

If we find one before our fuel runs out, we'll land. At that time, we'll figure out where we are and decide where we want to go next. Meanwhile, folks, just sit back, relax and enjoy your trip."

Would you enjoy your flight, or would you wish someone had taken the time to file a flight plan?

Although your plans may not be crystal clear and your goals are not in writing at this very moment, you are still, nonetheless, moving forward. As harsh as this may sound, you are where you are—who you are—and what you are because of choices you have made. Your past decisions and actions have placed you in your current circumstances.

If your decision (your goal) is to make just enough money to pay your bills, then your actions will generate the outcome. If your decision (goal) is to make it through the day until 5:00 p.m. so you can rush home to a drink in front of the TV, then you will probably accomplish that goal.

Conversely, if your decision is to achieve spiritual serenity, good health or long life, then you can achieve that too. And if your goal is financial independence, then nothing can stop you from reaching it. If you are truly committed, back your decision with a plan, and persist...persist...persist, you will eventually achieve your goal.

In a book called *The Joy of Working*, the authors describe what the late Henry Fonda once observed. He said that a thoroughbred horse never looks at the other racehorses. It just concentrates on running the fastest race it can. We have to fight the tendency to look at others to see how far they've come. The only thing that counts is how we use the potential we possess, and that we run our race to the best of our abilities.

Two Conditions for Your Success

A man came to America from Europe. After being processed at Ellis Island, he went into a cafeteria in New York City to get lunch. Sitting down at an empty table, he waited for someone to come over and take his order. Of course, nobody did. Finally, a kind man sat down next to him and explained how a cafeteria works.

"You go to that end of the line," he said, "and walk along, picking out what you want to eat. When you get to the other end, they'll tell you how much to pay for it."

Many years later, the immigrant was explaining to his teenage grandson about his first day in America. "I soon learned that's how everything works in this country. Life is a cafeteria here. You can get anything you want as long as you're willing to pay the price. You can even obtain success, but you'll never get it if you wait for someone to bring it to you. You have to get up and get it yourself."

The greatest ability man has over animals is that he can choose what he will surrender to, or what will be embraced and conquered. Humans were created with freewill. The problem is that most people never decide with absolute clarity, determination, and resolve what they truly want. It is essential, before traveling further on this journey, that you are aware of two requirements that must be met and accepted in order to enjoy the benefits of reaching your maximum potential.

Condition number one is **you are responsible**. Your acceptance of responsibility is the antecedent of establishing and setting your goals. Self-responsibility and goal setting go hand-in-hand.

People who are irresponsible always pack a suitcase full of excuses. An excuse is a belief that outside circumstances, someone else or something else is responsible for life's outcome. As Zig Ziglar says: "There is a disease that cripples greatness, and that is the disease of excusitis."

Granted, we all are not brought into this world under the same circumstances. We are born into different racial, ethnic and religious backgrounds. Some of us are short, some are tall. Some are beautiful and some are plain. While some are privileged, others are abused, abandoned or physically challenged. But, as Theodore Roosevelt once observed, so what? "You do what you can, with what you have, where you are."

It is natural to cling to and even covet your reasons for why it seems impossible to reach your maximum potential. However, these reasons won't help you reach your goals. Ernest Hemingway explained, "Do not think about the past. This is the time to think of what you can do with what there still is."

To test the validity of your excuses, ask yourself this question: Has there ever been, or is there now, anyone who has experienced the same problems and setbacks, yet succeeded despite the challenges? If you are able to answer yes and locate someone else who, in a similar or worse situation, was able to overcome in spite of the limitations, then your "reason" for not improving is just an excuse. What one person believed and achieved, you can do as well. Letting go of your excuses and accepting complete responsibility is one of the hardest challenges of life.

The second condition to effective goal setting is **you must resolve to pay the full price of greatness in advance.** You must sow before you reap. A farmer first plants the crop and then reaps the harvest. There is no reverse relationship to cause and effect. Frustration in the quest for excellence will come if you try to disrespect this immutable law.

You give before you get, you ask before you receive, and you must knock before the door will be opened. Simply put, sowing and reaping, cause and effect, dictate that first you pay the price, then you receive the reward.

What is the price? It has been said opportunity comes disguised, cleverly dressed, in work clothes. Most things worth achieving will require a sustained effort, so you should be prepared to work long and hard before you achieve your desired outcome.

Why Don't People Set Goals?

It is a tragedy to realize that very few people in today's society are setting goals. Statistics reveal that less than three percent of men and women have a defined life plan (goal). And fewer than one percent of those who do have goals, read and review them regularly.

What excuses do we use to keep us off track?

- **Ignorance is not bliss:** From preschool through obtaining a university degree, an individual is easily exposed to 16 to 18 years of formal education. Yet, very little education, if any, is given to the instruction of goal setting, even though it would prepare the graduate for achieving true happiness and success.

By the time you complete this chapter, you will be aware of the importance of setting and achieving goals. If you should decide not to establish them, then laziness and complacency are your new enemies.

- **Laziness and procrastination:** Robert Benchley once jokingly said, "I do most of my work sitting down. That's where I shine." Is that where you excel? There are talkers and there are doers. Though talkers want to be successful and improve their lives, they aren't willing to make the effort to change. You can wish, hope and pray for the future, but eventually you have to be on your feet to accomplish the feat. When you have something to do that is worthwhile, don't talk about it—do it. After you have done it, others will talk about it.

- **Reference group:** If you are involved in a social reference group in which there are no goals, you may naturally make the assumption that goal setting is not important. However, these people are like the boat and plane captain who go in *every* direction because they have *no* direction. Keep in mind there is a suction caused by those who drift backwards. Avoid them.

You can predict how far you will be in your life five years from now by two indexes. First, what are you putting into your mind? Second, what types of individuals are in your social circle?

- **Fear of failure:** Our fear of failure, of making a mistake, or encountering criticisms, is the primary reason we don't set goals.

Here are some thoughts on failure:

- ❑ The only time you don't want to fail is the last time you try.

- ❑ To be successful, you have to be willing to fail.

- ❑ Don't let failure become a habit.

- ❑ Lack of willpower and drive cause more failure than lack of imagination and ability.

- ❑ When you make a mistake, you can be dissatisfied without being discouraged.

Although everything changes, you are, in all probability, unable to effect many of the changes that are occurring. Therefore, the only way to manage your transformation is to control your reaction to these changes and how you, in turn, change yourself. The benefit of goals is that, by taking control of yourself, you supervise the metamorphosis that will occur in your life to overcome temporary failures.

We have all experienced the ridicule and laughter of others because we wanted to do something they can't even imagine doing. Then, when we try it and experience setbacks, they are at our elbows saying, "I told you so."

Leslie Bernard Kilgore had a dream about building a newspaper that would be available across the United States. He wanted to broaden its editorial content to include a financial trade sheet, believing it would appeal to everyone earning a living. Friends said it wouldn't catch on. Today, his dream is known as the *Wall Street Journal.*

Famed pilot Chuck Yeager wanted to fly faster than sound. In the 1940s, aeronautical engineers and physicists believed that no one could break the sound barrier. Yeager didn't listen and flew right through it.

A reporter asked George Bernard Shaw, shortly before Shaw died, to play the "What if" game. He said, "Mr. Shaw, you have visited with some of the most famous people in the world. You've known royalty, world-renowned authors, artists, teachers, and dignitaries from every part of the world. If you could live your life over and be anybody you've known, or any person from history, who would you choose to be?"

Shaw replied, "I would choose to be the man George Bernard Shaw could have been, but never was."

Don't let these influences keep you from being the person you were meant to be. Anne Frank, the German Jewish refugee and diarist, wrote, "Everyone has inside of him a piece of good news. The good news is that you don't know how great you can be! How much you can love! What you can accomplish! And what your potential is!"

Begin today to tap your potential. Here's how.

METHODS TO DEVELOP YOUR GOALS

Goals Must Be in Writing. If your goal is not in writing and placed within a time frame, it remains merely a wish. As best-selling business author Harvey Mackay says, "A goal is a dream with a deadline."

The primary reason people don't write down their goals is because of lack of commitment. Putting one's name on the dotted line signifies a commitment and builds a psychological obligation.

When you write each goal—the plans for achieving it, and a deadline—you usher in clarity and reality. Therefore, your goals should be precisely detailed. For example, if you want a new home, describe, in detail, how it will look. What is its location? How many bedrooms and baths? Does it have an office or a gym? How is it decorated, and what is the square footage? When you can visualize your goal, it becomes compelling.

Also, be sure to write your goals in the present tense as if already achieved. Not just, "I want a new home" but "I will be enjoying my new waterfront home by (date)." If your goal is a new automobile, describe it in detail in the present tense. "I am driving my new automobile. It is my favorite color, white with beige leather interior." Continue to elaborate every detail, feature and benefit until you bring your goal to life.

Decision and Desire. Complacency and fear are the root causes of selling yourself short of what you deserve. However, a concrete decision backed by an intense desire will cause you to take action. Motivation comes from within. You must develop strong reasons to keep your desire burning brightly.

The famous tightrope performer Karl Wallenda put it this way: "Being on the tightrope is living; everything else is waiting." That desire must motivate you enough to risk the walk.

Take the time to make a list of all the benefits that you will enjoy as a result of accomplishing your goal. The more benefits you identify, the more intense the desire; and a strong desire will keep you from being discouraged if the going gets rough—as it probably will. Picture yourself, like Wallenda, making it to the other side and hearing the applause.

Goals Are Personal. When establishing your goals, be sure that they are those you want for yourself, not goals someone else wants for you. You have every right to remain self-centered when determining what you want to be, to do or to have.

Clare Boothe Luce, one of the most successful women in America, author of articles, books, plays, twice elected to Congress, former ambassador to Italy, said, "I often thought that if I were to write an autobiography, my title would be 'The Autobiography of a Failure.'" When asked why she felt that way, she explained that all she had ever wanted to do was write, but she put aside her goals to satisfy the goals of others and, in doing so, failed to achieve her own.

Believe and You Will Receive. The Bible states, "Everything is possible for him who believes." You must have faith, prior to the journey, that it is possible for you to arrive at your final destination. You must also believe that you deserve your goals and that they will happen at the exact moments you are ready to receive them. Remember, God's delays are not His denials.

Goals Must Be Significant and Incremental. They should not be out of reach, but should stretch your abilities. If your goal is to lose weight, don't attempt to lose 20, 30 or 40 pounds overnight. Instead, set believable, incremental goals that will motivate and fuel your fires. Start with five pounds and, after that achievement, reset your goals for another five pounds. If your goal is beyond anything you have ever achieved in the past, setting it too high and trying to reach it too quickly may cause disillusionment and usher in discouragement. It's easy to quit unless you are experiencing success in measurable degrees.

If you want to increase your business, you must determine your business cycles and when a majority of the revenue is earned in a particular season. If your goal is to earn $100,000 per year, then reduce the aggregate to its lowest common denominator. $100,000 per year is $8,333 per month, $2,000 per week based on 50 weeks, $400 per day based on 250 work days, or $40 per hour based on a 10-hour day. From here on, only engage in $40-per-hour activities.

You've probably heard that the way to eat an elephant is one bite at a time. Or the way to move a mountain is one stone at a time. When a task seems insurmountable, break it down into smaller tasks. Set incremental goals. Then they become measurable, believable and achievable.

Determine Your Starting Point. To get where you are going, you must first determine where you are. If you want to lose weight, then first weigh yourself. If you want to increase your net worth, you must create a financial statement of your current liabilities and assets.

Keep in the forefront of your mind that what gets measured is what gets done, and analyzing your current position gives you a baseline from which to measure your progress.

Departing From Your Personal Comfort Zone. Whenever you embrace greatness, there is sacrifice involved. There is a price that must be paid, and the price must be paid in advance. What are you willing to either start doing or stop doing? And are you willing to pay the price?

When Julius Ceasar sailed across the channel from Gaul and landed with his legions in what is now England, what did he do to ensure the success of his army? He halted his soldiers on the cliffs and, when they looked 200 feet below them, they saw every one of the ships that had carried them across the channel completely ablaze. They were now stranded in enemy territory, with no link to their own country, and no means of retreat. What else could they do but advance? What else could they do but conquer? What else could they do but fight with every ounce of strength that was in their souls? And that is precisely what they did.

Your past is a burned ship. All the faults, failures, and memories should be set ablaze. You cannot retreat into that comfort zone anymore, because victory awaits over the hill. In the future, it will be time for you to embrace your own form of greatness.

List Your Obstacles. If there are no obstacles, you probably do not have a worthwhile goal, but merely an activity. Your obstacle may be external, such as your involvement in a bad relationship or job. External obstacles are easier to correct. It's just a decision to let go, handle the consequences, and move on. However, internal obstacles are more difficult to confront. If your internal obstacle is a lack of skill, for example, you may have to sacrifice evenings to obtain an education. If your obstacle is a destructive habit, then you must be willing to work toward breaking it.

Whose Help Do You Need? List all of those whose cooperation you may need. No one does it alone. Everyone needs someone. The rule in obtaining cooperation is to be a "go-giver," not a "go-getter." The most successful people are those who have helped other people obtain the things they want. This takes us back to the principle of sowing and reaping. If you take every opportunity to help others, others will help you.

Goals Must Have Deadlines. What is the exact time, day, week, month and year you will achieve your goal? There are tangible goals and intangible goals. Tangible goals are those you experience with one of the senses. You can touch, taste, smell, see or hear it. When establishing timelines for tangible goals, you activate a "pressure system" which ensures accomplishment. The most common reason people don't set deadlines is that they fear they will not accomplish their goals. So, what if you set a deadline and don't achieve it by that date? Fine. You still will have made progress. Simply establish another timeline.

As Henry David Thoreau asked many years ago, "Did you ever hear of a man who had striven all his life faithfully and singly toward an object, and in no measure obtained it? If a man constantly aspires, is he not elevated? Did ever a man try heroism, magnanimity, truth, sincerity, and find that there was no advantage in them ...that it was a vain endeavor?"

Are your goals intangible, such as developing new habits and disciplines? Be patient. It took relentless, forced repetition to develop the bad habit in the first place. Incidentally, the word discipline is derived from the root word disciple, which means a devoted student and follower. You are a devoted follower of your goals. You are also a student, learning as you progress. Be kind to yourself as you gradually identify and abandon destructive habits. And remember... you can do it!

Review and Rehearse Your Goals. View your goals with clear mental pictures, as if they were already achieved. Each time you visit and revisit your goals, you increase your belief and faith. Etch your goals deep into your subconscious by reviewing them repeatedly. **As you think, so you are.**

Take Action. Take action, but realize situations and circumstances will never be perfect. Get started where you are with what you have. The hardest part is always the first step.

Achieve Balance. You need goals in all areas of your life. Just as scales must be balanced to properly weigh, you must have your goals aligned so you'll be properly balanced. You need spiritual goals, family goals, career goals, health goals, financial goals and goals for intellectual development.

In achieving balance, you are constantly working on something important to you. When you're not working on your career, you invest your time with your family. And when you're with your family, you can invest time developing your spiritual goals. Of course you need time alone to invest in physical fitness and in contemplation of your life. Your true mission is to realize continuous achievement in all areas of your life.

Telling People About Your Goals. Keep your goals confidential. Avoid telling everyone what you are planning. This is not to contradict point number nine (obtaining help from other people). It's just that there are those who will slap you with criticism and intimidate with laughter, because you dare to change...dare to achieve something beyond their dreams. The rule in telling others is this: If it's a career goal, such as being the number one salesperson, tell only those who will encourage you, like your manager or spouse or others who will act as a coach to cheer you onward. If it's a personal improvement goal, such as losing weight or quitting smoking, then ask your friends for support. This will also create pressure for you to follow through.

You should be willing to encourage those who share their goals with you, too. When you tell others they can do it—that they deserve it and to go for it—the law of sowing and reaping kicks in and you will reap a richer harvest than you could ever give away.

Persistence. Winning is a habit. Unfortunately, so is quitting. If you tenaciously persist, you will succeed. When you reach the end of your rope, tie a knot and climb upward. You will eventually reach the top.

FOUR-STEP FORMULA FOR GOAL SETTING

STEP 1

We are now going to make the invisible visible and help make your dreams a reality in critical areas of your life. Elevate your thinking, think big thoughts and begin to make decisions as you explore the possibilities of your life.

I. FINANCIAL & CAREER GOALS

Write everything you would like to have happen in your career and financial life. What do you want to be and how much do you want to earn?

A. DO YOU WANT TO EARN...

A. _____ Per year?

B. $ 50,000 Per year?

C. $ 75,000 Per year?

D. $100,000 Per year?

E. _____ Per year?

F. $1,000,000 Per year?

G. _____ Per year?

NOTE: *A rule of thumb is that increases of 10 percent to 50 percent are believable within your deepest subconscious level. If you are currently earning $50,000, it may be hard for you to believe with absolute conviction the possibility of earning $100,000. But an increase of 50 percent, a raise from $50,000 to $75,000, is believable, highly probable and may be accomplished by simply changing jobs. After you reach $75,000, it's just a matter of readjusting up-ward.*

B. WHAT ABOUT YOUR FINANCIAL WORTH?

How much will you save this year?_____

How much will you save in two years?_____

How much will you save in five years?_____

When do you want to retire? _____

What will your net worth be? _____

C. WHAT ARE YOU CURRENTLY DOING TO MANAGE YOUR MONEY?

Do you have an accountant?_____

Do you have a savings account?_____

Do you have a tax account?_____

Do you have a mutual fund?_____

Do you have a retirement account?_____

Do you have a college savings fund?_____

Other_____

_____

D. WHAT ARE YOUR CAREER GOALS?

Would you like to be a manager? Top salesperson? What do you want to be? Describe your ideal position.

_____

_____

_____

_____

_____

How would you like to be recognized within your profession?

_____

_____

What do you or can you contribute?_____

_____

_____

Is your current position taking you where you want to be?

_____

How many hours per day/per week do you want to work?

_____

NOTE: *The preceding questions are examples. Create your own questions and decide specifically what it is you want to achieve.*

II. FAMILY GOALS

A. HOW MUCH TIME DO YOU WANT TO INVEST WITH YOUR FAMILY?

❑ Do you have a specific family day?

❑ Have you taken your spouse or significant other on a date?

❑ Are you participating with your children's sports activities?

❑ Are you and your family working toward a goal together?

Note: It's amazing how much time is spent planning the wedding, versus planning the marriage.

❑ Where do you want to live?

❑ What does your new home look like?

❑ How would you like your family to remember you?

246

B. HOW MUCH TIME DO YOU WANT TO TAKE OFF?

- ❏ Do you want evenings off?
- ❏ Can you reduce your work week from six to five days?
- ❏ Where and when do you want to vacation?
- ❏ Have you ever dreamed of traveling cross-country?
- ❏ What exotic location would you like to visit?

III. SPIRITUAL AND INTELLECTUAL GOALS

A. HOW CAN YOU DEVELOP YOUR SPIRITUAL PERSON?

- ❏ Do you want to attend services or meetings?
- ❏ Do you want to contribute financially to a church or charity?
- ❏ Volunteer your time?
- ❏ Visit prisons, shelters, or homes?

B. ARE YOU GROWING INTELLECTUALLY?

- ❏ How much television do you watch?
- ❏ Will you commit to personal development?
- ❏ Are you willing to study in your field one hour per day?
- ❏ Does your local college offer extension courses?
- ❏ What new skills do you need to develop?
- ❏ Do you want to learn:

  To speak a foreign language?
  To dance or play an instrument?
  To speak in public?
  To become computer literate?
  Other:_____

IV. HEALTH

- ❑ What are you doing to create the body you desire?
- ❑ Are you a member of a gym?
- ❑ Will you invest in a home gym?
- ❑ Will you change your diet?
- ❑ Do you need to rise one hour earlier to accomplish exercise?
- ❑ What weight are you committed to achieving?
- ❑ What size are you in the future?

V. DISCRETIONARY GOALS

A. WOULD YOU LIKE TO...

- ❑ Attend a Broadway play?
- ❑ Attend a professional sports event?
- ❑ Take tennis lessons?
- ❑ Learn to fly?
- ❑ Preach a life-changing sermon?
- ❑ Have lunch with a famous person?
- ❑ Other_____

B. WHAT KINDS OF TOYS DO YOU WANT?

- ❑ Vacation home?
- ❑ Boat?
- ❑ Sports car?
- ❑ Jet plane?
- ❑ Jewelry and accessories?
- ❑ What does your new wardrobe look like?

C. WOULD YOU LIKE TO START...

- ❏ An art collection?

- ❏ A coin or stamp collection?

- ❏ Other?

STEP 2

SELECTING YOUR GOALS

After creating your list, select one major goal in each of the following categories: Health, Family, Spiritual, Career, Financial, Personal Development, and Discretionary. One goal in each category is plenty to start. As you achieve sustained success with the one goal, come back to your list or create a new list and select another goal. Success will breed success and, as you develop your goal-setting muscles, you will eventually be able to balance multiple goals in each category.

Write your goal in the present tense, as if already achieved, and the date of its achievement. Then list carefully the reasons why it is important to you. The more benefits you list the stronger your motivation.

HEALTH

Goal _____ Date_____
Reasons of importance:

FAMILY

Goal_____Date_____
Reasons of importance:

SPIRITUAL

Goal _____Date_____
Reasons of importance:

CAREER

Goal_____Date_____

Reasons of importance:

FINANCIAL

Goal_____Date_____

Reasons of importance:

PERSONAL DEVELOPMENT

Goal_____Date_____

Reasons of importance:

DISCRETIONARY (Toys & Adventure)

Goals_____ Date_____

Reasons of importance:

STEP 3

IDENTIFY YOUR ROAD BLOCKS

List the limiting factors or challenges to the achievement of your goals. What one thing would keep you from your success and how will you overcome it?

> NOTE: *The limiting factor may be internal and involve change. If so, what will you sacrifice?*

Health_____

_____

Family_____

_____

Spiritual_____

_____

Career_____

_____

Financial_____

_____

Personal Development_____

_____

Discretionary_____

_____

STEP 4

DEVELOP YOUR ACTION PLAN

Effective goal setting requires you to start with the end result in mind and work your way backward to today. In other words, if you set a yearly goal, what action steps will you take on a daily, weekly, monthly, and quarterly basis to insure your desired outcome?

WHAT ACTION DO I PLAN TO TAKE TO MAKE MY ONE-YEAR GOALS A REALITY?

A—**Daily:** What action steps must I implement on a daily basis to achieve my weekly goals?

HEALTH: Action steps_____

_____

FAMILY: Action steps_____

_____

SPIRITUAL: Action steps_____

_____

CAREER: Action steps_____

_____

FINANCIAL: Action steps_____

_____

PERSONAL DEVELOPMENT: Action steps_____

_____

DISCRETIONARY: Action steps_____

_____

B—Weekly:What action steps must I implement on a weekly basis to achieve my monthly goals?

HEALTH: Action steps_____

_____

FAMILY: Action steps_____

_____

SPIRITUAL: Action steps_____

_____

CAREER: Action steps_____

_____

FINANCIAL: Action steps_____

_____

PERSONAL DEVELOPMENT: Action steps_____

_____

DISCRETIONARY: Action steps_____

_____

C—**Monthly:** What action steps must I implement on a monthly basis to achieve my quarterly goals?

HEALTH: Action steps_____

FAMILY: Action steps_____

SPIRITUAL: Action steps_____

CAREER: Action steps_____

FINANCIAL: Action steps_____

PERSONAL DEVELOPMENT: Action steps_____

_____

DISCRETIONARY: Action steps_____

_____

D—**Quarterly:** What action steps must I implement on a quarterly basis to achieve my yearly goals?

HEALTH: Action steps_____

FAMILY: Action steps_____

SPIRITUAL: Action steps_____

CAREER: Action steps_____

FINANCIAL: Action steps_____

PERSONAL DEVELOPMENT: Action steps_____

_____

DISCRETIONARY: Action steps_____

2 YEARS—What or where do I want to be in two years?

HEALTH: Action steps_____

FAMILY: Action steps_____

SPIRITUAL: Action steps_____

CAREER: Action steps_____

FINANCIAL: Action steps_____

PERSONAL DEVELOPMENT: Action steps_____

_____

DISCRETIONARY: Action steps_____

_____

5 YEARS—What or where do I want to be in five years? What do I want to accomplish in five years?

HEALTH: Action steps_____

FAMILY: Action steps_____

SPIRITUAL: Action steps_____

CAREER: Action steps_____

FINANCIAL: Action steps_____

PERSONAL DEVELOPMENT: Action steps_____

_____

DISCRETIONARY: Action steps_____

_____

Two final thoughts:

The privilege of a lifetime is being who you are. Make the most of it.
If there were dreams for sale, which ones would you buy?

Recommended Resources

This bibliography contains most of the research and resources used in writing this book. I highly recommend you include the following titles in your personal success library.

Advanced Selling Strategies, Brian Tracy, Simon & Schuster Inc., 1995

The Official Handbook for New Home Salespeople, Bob Schultz, New Home Specialist, 1998

New Home Marketing, Dave Stone, Dearborn Press, 1989

Secrets of the Superstars, Bonnie Alfried, Bonnie Alfried and Associates, 1993

How to Master the Art of Selling, Tom Hopkins, Warner books, 1982

If it Ain't Broke...Break it, Robert J. Kriegel and Louis Patler, Warner Books, 1991

Closing Strong, Myers Barnes, Myers Barnes Associates Inc., 1997

The Sales Closing Book, Gerhard Gschwandtner, Personal Selling Power, 1988

The Sales Script Book, Gerhard Gschwandtner and Donald J. Moire, Ph.D., Personal Selling Power, 1986

Smart Selling Techniques, Bob Schultz, New Home Specialist, 1997

Spin Selling, Neil Rackham, McGraw Hill, 1988

Dig Your Well Before You Are Thirsty, Harvey Mackay, Doubleday, 1997

Video Cassettes

Handling Objections, Jack and Jerry Kinder, Nightingale Conant

How to Become a Real Estate Superstar, Mike Ferry, Mike Ferry Productions

The Psychology of Success, Brian Tracy, Brian Tracy International

Sell More New Homes, Nicki Joy, Nicki Joy and Associates

38 Proven Ways to Close that Sale, Marc Victor Hansen, Career Trac Publications

24 Techniques for Closing the Sale, Brian Tracy, Nightingale Conant

Negotiate Like the Pros, John Patrick Dolen, Career Trac Publications

Audio Cassettes

The Psychology of Selling, Brian Tracy, Nightingale Conant

The Secrets of Power Negotiating, Roger Dawson, Nightingale Conant

Hardball, Robert L. Shook, Nightingale Conant

Follow Up: And Turn Your Contacts Into Contracts, Myers Barnes, Myers Barnes Associates Inc.

The Five Minute Professional, Bob Schultz, New Home Specialist

For Your Continuing Education

The Greatest Salesman in the World, Og Mandino, Bantum Books

How to Market Through Direct Mail, Nido Qubein, Nightingale Conant

How I Raised Myself from Failure to Success, Frank Bettger, Prentice Hall

The Closers, Ben Gay, Hampton House Publications, Inc.

A Whack on the Side of the Head, Roger Von Oech, Warner Books

The Platinum Rule, Tony Alessandra, Ph.D. and Michael J. O'Connor, Ph.D., Warner Books

Expanding Your Thinking, Mike Ferry, Mike Ferry Productions

Low Profile Selling, Tom Hopkins, Nightingale Conant

Instant Influence, Robert Cialdini, Dartnell

Rocking the Ages, J. Walker Smith, Anne Cluman, Harper Business

Conceptual Selling, Robert B. Miller, Stephen Eheiman, Tad Tileja, Warner Books

How to be a Great Communicator, Nido Qubein, Executive Press

The Power of Your Subconscious Mind, Dr. Joseph Murphy, Prentice Hall, Inc.

Sell Your Way to the Top, Zig Ziglar, Nightingale Conant

The Psychology of Winning, Denis Waitley, Nightingale Conant

How to Sell at Prices Higher Than Your Competition, Lawrence L. Steinmetz, Ph.D.

The Millionaire Next Door, Thomas J. Stanley, Ph.D., William D. Danko, Ph.D., Longstreet Press

Selling Power Magazine, Gerhard Gschwandtner

Builder Magazine, National Association of Home Builders

Go for the Magic, Pat Williams, Thomas Nelson Publishers

Relationship Selling, Jim Cathcart, Perigee

Professional Builder Magazine, Cahners

INDEX

ABOUT THE AUTHOR

MYERS BARNES is regarded as one of America's top professional speakers and seminar leaders. Driven by the virtues of personal development and excellence, his impact in the fields of human potential and sales achievement has been far reaching.

As a licensed general contractor and broker, Myers has and continues to "walk the talk." He climbed the "ladder" from salesperson to sales manager to Vice President of Sales for a real estate development company. Today his hobby is his vocation. Myers teaches countless people every year how to reach their own extraordinary potential by mastering the art of New Home and Neighborhood Sales.

In addition to *Reach the Top in New Home and Neighborhood Sales*, Myers is also the acclaimed author of *Closing Strong, the Super Sales Handbook* and the audio and video training tapes, *Follow-Up*. As a noted author, Myers has produced articles for many of the nation's top sales-related magazines and trade publications. He maintains an active position on the Executive Advisory Board for The Fisher Institute for Professional Selling, University of Akron, Ohio.

Do you have questions about your sales career? Myers is always eager to help others reach the top. For a personal response, write or e-mail him at the address printed below.

For corporate or group consulting services, training programs, seminars or presentations, please write, call or e-mail:

Myers Barnes Associates Inc.
Post Office Box 50
Kitty Hawk, NC 27949
Phone (252) 261-7611, Fax (252) 261-7615
E-mail: sellmore@myersbarnes.com